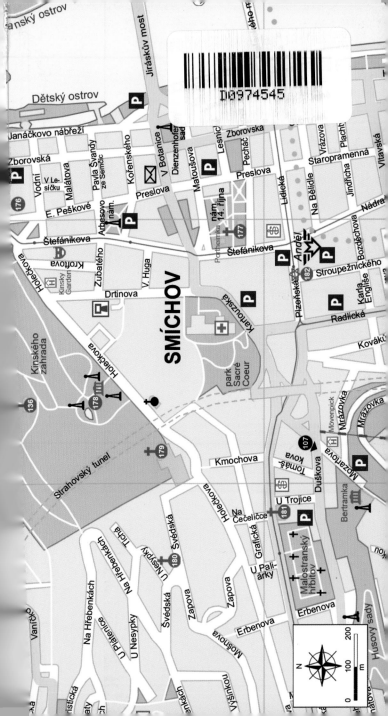

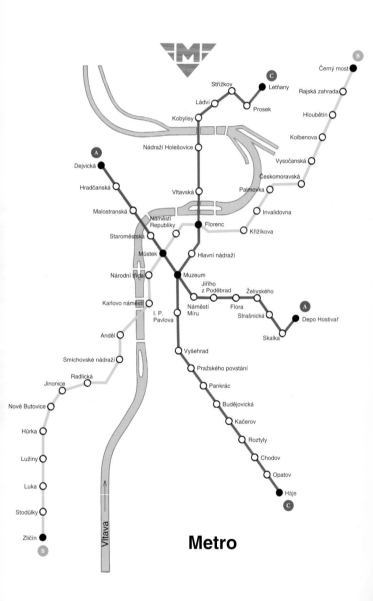

Metro

Prague

A Guide to the Golden City

by Harald Salfellner

Vitalis

The author,
Dr Harald Salfellner

(born in 1962), studied medicine in Graz and Prague and has lived in the Czech capital since 1989 as an editor, publisher, and author. He has published a series of essays and articles as well as books about Prague, some of which have been translated into a variety of languages (among them *Franz Kafka and Prague*, *The Golden Lane*, *Mozart and Prague*, *Das Palais Lobkowicz*, *Prague under Water* and *Prague Cafés*).

Contents

Prague – *A Guide*

★ The ten most famous sights in Prague at a glance:

★ The recommended public transport links may represent just one of many options to get to the respective sights.
Ⓜ Metro   Ⓣ Tram   Ⓑ Bus

★ A much more comprehensive publication than this little travel companion would be required to present all the beauty and sights of Prague. Thus, the book in hand contains only a selection intended to stimulate further study. However, Vitalis Publishers offer an extensive collection of Prague literature to assist the interested reader in gaining a profound understanding of the Golden City of Prague.

★ Where it was not provided by the author himself, the photographic material in this book has been taken from the publisher's archive of photographs and historical publications.

★ 1ˢᵗ May 2009

© Vitalis, 2009 • Translated from the German original by Monica Sperling • Produced in the European Union • ISBN 978-80-7253-296-4 • www.vitalis-verlag.com • All rights reserved

A Brief National History

4th century BC
The Celtic Boii settle in Bohemia.

3rd–7th centuries AD
Germanic and Slavic tribes settle in the country.

7th century AD
Foundation of a tribal association by Franconian trader Samo.

9th century AD
Era of the Great Moravian Empire; the Czech clans come under the leadership of the Přemyslid dynasty.
Legendary age of the prophetess Libuše.
Era of Bořivoj I, the first Czech Prince to be baptized (with his wife Ludmila). The royal seat is transferred to Prague Castle.

10th century AD
Prague comes under the bishopric of Regensburg and develops into a significant trading city. Prince Wenceslas [Václav] I (the saint) rules under German fiefdom until his assassination (935) by his brother Boleslav I.
In 973 AD Prague is elevated to a bishopric under the archbishopric of Mainz.
993 AD: Foundation of the still existing Benedictine monastery of Břevnov by Bishop Adalbert [Vojtěch].

1085
Vratislav II (as King Vratislav I) is the first Bohemian Duke to be granted the status of kingship by Emperor Henry IV.

1212
King Frederick II bestows the privilege of a hereditary kingship on Přemysl Otakar II ("The Sicilian Golden Bull").

1278
King Přemysl Otakar II, under whose reign Bohemia grew into a powerful kingdom, is defeated by Rudolph I of Habsburg in the battle of the Marchfeld.

1306
With the assassination of Wenceslas III in Olomouc, the Přemyslid dynasty dies out after losing its last male heir to the throne.

1310–1437
The House of Luxembourg takes over the Bohemian throne.

1344
Prague is elevated to an archbishopric.

1346
Charles IV of Luxembourg becomes king; in 1355 he is crowned Holy Roman Emperor. Under his reign, the late medieval city experiences a period of extraordinary prosperity.

1348
Foundation of the first university north of the Alps and east of the Rhine.

Veduta of Prague in Schedel's World Chronicle (1493).

1356
Charles IV settles the election of the Emperor with the Golden Bull.

1378
Wenceslas IV succeeds the deceased Charles IV as king. A period of social, or rather, national unrest between Germans and Czechs begins. John of Nepomuk is drowned in the Vltava in 1393.

1409
As a consequence of the Kuttenberg Decrees, a large number of German students and professors leave the Charles University of Prague.

1415
Reformer Jan Hus is burned at the stake in Constance.

1419
First Defenestration of Prague (from the New Town City Hall). Beginning of the Hussite wars, characterised by religious, social and national dissent.

1420
The radical Hussites led by Jan Žižka triumph over Emperor Si-

Burning of Jan Hus at the stake in Constance.

A Brief National History

gismund at Vítkov Hill near
Prague.

1434
In the battle of Lipany, moderate
Hussites and Imperial troops win
a joint victory over the radical
Taborite People's Army.

1458–1471
Era of the elected King George
of Poděbrady [Jiří z Poděbrad].

1471–1526
Period of the Polish-Lithuanian
Jagiellonian dynasty. The last
scion of the Jagiellonians, King
Louis II, loses his life in the battle of Mohács against the Turks.
The Crownlands of Bohemia
(and Hungary) come under the
rule of the House of Habsburg.

1526–1564
Reign of Ferdinand I of Habsburg. During his reign the Jesuits
are summoned to Prague.

Execution of the Bohemian gentlemen
in front of the Old Town Hall.

1526–1612
Reign of Emperor Rudolph II of
Habsburg; Prague becomes the
capital of the Holy Roman Empire, and its hub of arts and sciences, once again.

1618
Second Defenestration of Prague,
marking the beginning of the
Thirty Years' War.

1620
The Protestant Bohemian estates
are defeated by the Catholic
league at the Battle of White
Mountain. The consequences are
a thorough counter-reformation,
dispossession and banishment of
the established aristocracy.

1621
27 Ringleaders of the rebellious
estates – Germans and Czechs –
are executed on the Old Town
Square.

Emperor Rudolph II (J. Heintz c. 1594).

At the court of Rudolph II: jesters, scholars, artists.

1634
General Albrecht von Wallenstein is murdered in Cheb.

1648
Swedish troops occupy the Lesser Town and Prague Castle. The Thirty Years' War ends with the Peace of Westphalia.

1721
Canonization of the Bohemian martyr John of Nepomuk.

1740–1780
Reign of Empress Maria Theresa; Prague is besieged several times during the Wars of Succession.

1780–1790
Reign of the reformist Emperor Joseph II, era of mainly social, political and religious reforms, dissolution of numerous monasteries.

1784
The union of the four towns of Prague forms a metropolis of more than 70,000 inhabitants.

1787
Mozart's first visit to Prague; premiere of his opera *Don Giovanni* at the Estates Theatre.

1792–1835
Reign of Emperor Francis II; Napoleon's troops in Prague, Metternich suppresses endeavours for democratic freedom during the period of the Restoration.

1845
Establishment of the Vienna–Prague railway line; trade and industry flourish in consequence.

W. A. Mozart (by Barbara Krafft).

Emperor Francis Joseph I.

The first president of Czechoslovakia: T. G. Masaryk.

1848
Civil Revolution, Slavic Congress led by František Palacký.
Ascension to the throne of Emperor Francis Joseph I, who forges the destiny of the monarchy until his demise in 1916.

1861
The German townsmen lose their majority in the city council of Prague.

1866
The predominance of Germany over her rival Austria is cemented by the former's victory on the battlefield of Königgrätz.

1882
Charles University is divided into separate German and Czech universities.

1891
The Jubilee National Exhibition provides an opportunity for Bohemia to present itself as a highly developed industrial state.

1897
Severe anti-German violence in the streets of Prague.

1918
End of the First World War, founding of the republic with Tomáš Garrigue Masaryk as its first president.

1920
The constitution of Czechoslovakia comes into effect. Prague becomes a modern capital.

1938
Munich Agreement: annexation of the German-populated Sudetenland to the German Reich.

The Swastika marching into Prague.

1939
German units march into the remaining Czech territory, the so-called "Rump Czechoslovakia". Establishment of the Reich Protectorate of Bohemia-Moravia under German rule.

1942
The assassination of Deputy Reich Protector Reinhard Heydrich by soldiers of the Czechoslovakian foreign army in exile triggers off the so-called "Heydrichiad" with brutal acts of retribution by the occupation forces.

1945–1946
On the basis of the so-called "Beneš Decrees", about three million citizens of German origin are expelled from Czechoslovakia; a large number of Sudeten Germans lose their lives.

Workers' militias march in support of the communist takeover.

Prague does not escape the Second World War unscathed.

1948
Communist coup d'état in Czechoslovakia, Klement Gottwald becomes president of the so-called "People's Republic" (ČSR).

1960
The ČSSR constitution is passed.

1968
The communist reformer Alexander Dubček and the reform movement "Prague Spring" succumb to the tanks of the Warsaw Pact.

1945
The Prague rebellion between the 5th and the 9th of May seals the end of the "Protectorate" era and claims many lives.

1969
Student Jan Palach dies by self-immolation at Wenceslas Square as a protest against the oppression of his people.

Prague Spring – tanks in Prague once again.

1974
The first underground train (metro) goes into service in Prague.

1977
The civil rights movement Charta 77 establishes itself as an opposition power.

1989
Thousands of citizens of the GDR seek refuge in the West German Embassy in Prague and eventually get to leave their

Citizens of the GDR escape over the fence into the FRG Embassy.

country to the West. The "Velvet Revolution" brings about the end of the communist regime; the dramatist Václav Havel is elected president.

1993
Following the disintegration of Czechoslovakia, the Czech and Slovak Republics emerge as independent nations.

Dissident und president Václav Havel.

1999
The Czech Republic joins NATO.

2002
A disastrous flood devastates large parts of the country and the inner city of Prague.

2003
Václav Klaus becomes the second president of the Czech Republic.

2004
The Czech Republic becomes a member of the European Union.

The City on the Vltava

The cityscape of Prague is fundamentally shaped by the Vltava: Altogether 17 bridges span the river, the oldest and best known of them being Charles Bridge. (In the foreground: a government building right at the riverside, close to Mánes Bridge).

Thanks to Smetana's symphonic poetry, the Vltava is perhaps one of the best known rivers in the world, although by world standards it is rather a humble rivulet: for the 31 km for which it flows through Prague, the average depth is about 4 m. Nonetheless, it is deep enough to be plied by all kinds of vehicles: excursion ships cruise past the world famous sights, chug towards Roztoky or to Prague Zoo, reaching the Slapy Dam, the Vtava's last large weir before Prague, only four hours after leaving the city centre. Humble though this rivulet may be, the Prague Steamship Company [Pražská paroplavební společnost] makes a livelihood plying its trade under the 17 bridges of Prague. The company's oldest and largest ship, the saloon paddle-steamer Vyšehrad, 62 m in length, ploughed through the Vltava's waves even before the Second World War. The first Bohemian paddle-steamer is, of course, no longer in use: the 38 m long

"Bohemia", with capacity for 140 passengers, designed by the industrialist Vojtěch Lanna and built by the Karlín Engineering Works, Prague, was launched on the 1st May 1841. The first cruise undertaken by this 32 horse-power ship, a technical masterpiece in its day, was downstream to the beautiful wine-producing town of Mělník, where the Vltava eventually merges with the Elbe River, ultimately emerging along with it into the sea. On the subject of the sea: Until recently, the Czech Navigation Company [Česká námořní plavba] was based in Prague with its 20 or more offshore ships despite the fact that its fleet could, of course, never sail into its home port of Prague. In the meantime, however, the ships have been sold.

Every proper waterway needs islands, and there are eight within the city of Prague, as well as the Kampa peninsula. One of these islands is **Marksman's Island** [Střelecký ostrov], which served as a training ground for archers in the Middle Ages. A wreath-laying ceremony takes place on the Smíchov embankment on **Children's Island** [Dětský ostrov]

In the summer the Vltava can be explored by pedal- or rowing boats – private boat rentals can be found close to Charles Bridge, for example.

The paddle-steamer Šumava cruises under Mánes Bridge.

The restaurant-ship Matylda at Rašinovo Quay prepares for the evening guests.

every year. This act of commemoration for those drowned in the river is performed at the allegorical statue of the River Vltava with the four maidens symbolising the tributaries Berounka, Sázava, Lužnice and Otava.

Sophie's Island [Žofín], also known as **Slavic Island**, was formed by alluvium in the

18th century, parallel to the National Theatre. Who could have imagined that this small river islet would, in 1841, be the site of the first steam engine in Prague, puffing and hissing round a circular wooden track for 150 m? Now, as then, Slavic Island is a venue for cultural events, balls, meetings, etc. Tourists can rent out rowing boats here and gain some experience as captains on the Vltava.

Hunter's Island [Štvanice], which now hosts a winter sport stadium, is older. It owes its name to the drive-hunts that once were held here.

Anybody who enjoys a maritime atmosphere should stroll down the embankment to the jetties and soak up the vibrant activity and port life that has developed there; restaurant ships and so-called botels (hotels on ships) are anchored here, small cafés beckon from the riverbanks, travel agents on the lookout for clients, freshwater sailors and tourist guides wait for the next excursion ship to dock. Here too, we are constantly greeted with the lovely cry of "Ahoj!"– there can be no doubt that "Bohemia lies by the sea".

A unique view of the Vltava opens up from shipboard: Excursion boats call at the Old Town embankment at Slavic Island [Slovanský ostrov], at Čech Bridge [Čechův most], and also south of Jirásek Bridge [Jiráskuv most].

A ride on the old paddle-steamer Vyšehrad (see below) is a special treat; it cruises between Rašinovo Quay and Čech Bridge. For more information, refer to the website at www.paroplavba.cz.

Prague Under Water

Charles Bridge threatened by floods.

On 12th August 2002, an unexpected tidal wave reaches the city of Prague. Karlín, Libeň, the Lesser Town – within a few hours, entire districts are submerged in the murky floods, people and animals succumb to the flood, irreplaceable valuables and cultural assets are destroyed. Prague residents – along with millions of people all over the world – wait with bated breath: Prague is under water. Tens of thousands of people are evacuated during the flood; thousands of people – police, soldiers and civilians – are deployed to help. Historic architecture is endangered, the first buildings collapse. Among the most drastically affected institutions is Prague Zoo, which is completely cut off. The animals are evacuated, but not all can be brought to safety. A hippopotamus, a bear, a lion and the bull elephant Kadir have to be put down. For several days, the European media reports on the fate of Gaston, a seal,

Franz Kafka is also up to his neck in water.

which escapes into the River Elbe from the Vltava and makes it all the way to Saxony before swimming into a German veterinary surgeon's net near Lutherstadt Wittenberg. But alas, it's a story without a happy ending. Gaston dies of exhaustion and stress on the return journey to Prague.

The flooded metro stations prove particularly problematic. Large parts of the public transportation service come to a standstill and remain severely impeded for months. The few trams still running are crammed full to the brim and cannot really replace the cancelled underground trains.

Apart from the tremendous material damage throughout the country, estimated at about 100 billion crowns, irreplaceable damage is done to cultural heritage in the city centre: the National Theatre, the Rudolfinum and the Jewish Museum are affected as well as several theatres and many private cultural institutions. Thus, more than half a million valuable books and innumerable papers and documents from the archives are irretrievably lost.

It takes almost a week before the water ebbs away and the clearing up can commence, but the affected areas of the city are like ghost towns for months to come.

After the water ebbs away the extent of the damage becomes evident.

The Lesser Town was worst affected.

Parks and Gardens in Prague

A sea of flowers at the Vojan Gardens [Vojanovy sady] in the Lesser Town.

The funicular at Petřín Hill.

Prague's gardens and parks are a world of their own! First of all, there are the ornamental gardens of the various palaces of the nobility: the Wallenstein and Czernin Gardens, the Palace Gardens of Kolowrat, Fürstenberg, Ledebour, Vrtba, Pállfy, Thun-Hohenstein, not forgetting, the garden of Lobkovicz Palace, so steeped in history. Some of these gardens are either closed to the public or only open on specific occasions. That is not the case with the Royal Gardens behind and below Prague Castle. Kafka liked to go for walks in the **Chotek Gardens** [Chotkovy sady] behind the Belvedere summer residence. Lovers of literature can gaze at the monument erected there in honour of the Czech poet Julius Zeyer. Only a stone's throw away there is a paradise for joggers and skaters: the numerous leisure time facilities in the **Letná Park** range from a children's playground to a beer-garden, and in summer, its shady tree-lined avenues attract young and old alike.

Further away from the city centre, on the busy Plzeňská Street, you reach **Cibulka**, an English landscape garden created in the 19th century. It was established thanks to Bishop Leopold Thun-Hohenstein, from Passau. He also had a folly built, along with a Chinese pavilion, an alpine cottage, a neo-Gothic forester's house and a hermitage complete with (mechanical) hermits. Naturally, a brook, a waterfall and a grotto also had to be included.

Also on Plzeňská Street lies the **Klamovka**, a former rural estate within a park complex.

The name harks back to the House of Clam-Gallas. Here too, a neo-Gothic gallery, a Rococo chapel and a pavilion remind one of better times, but the little park, which is home to a simple restaurant with a public garden, is still a popular destination for residents of the surrounding areas.

In the west of Prague lies **Břevnov Monastery** with its 18th-century gardens, the little castle Vojtěška and a miraculous spring. A short tram-ride further from the centre brings you to the **Star Game Enclosure** [obora Hvězda], in which Emperor Ferdinand I ordered a unique star-shaped Renaissance palace to be built. The leisure park with its walkways and benches was laid out in 1797.

A view of the Royal Gardens behind Prague Castle.

In the Arboretum [Stromovka].

Petřín Hill is also well worth a visit: this park complex, accessible from the Lesser Town, contains quiet nooks and promenades, rose gardens, old trees and flower beds, as well as monuments, sights and numerous amusements. A funicular leads from the Lesser Town up to the iron observation tower.

With an expanse of over a million square metres, the **Royal Enclosure** [Královská obora], also known as the **Arboretum** [Stromovka], is the largest park of the metropolis. Originally private property of the Bohemian kings, Přemysl Otakar II established a game enclosure here. It was said that even camels

Strolling through the Royal Gardens; St Vitus' Cathedral in the background.

were to be encountered within its boundaries! Until the 18th century, the Arboretum was linked to Prague Castle by an avenue of chestnut trees. This was cleared, however, during the Napoleonic Wars. The Arboretum has been a popular destination with Prague residents since 1850, when it was transformed into a park. The Prague Exhibition Grounds are also situated here, housing the popular panoramic picture of the Hussite Battle of Lipany (1434), a highly important event in Czech national history. From there, it is not far to Prague Zoo and the magnificent Baroque Chateau Troja.

Vladislav Jagiello's **Governor's summer palace** is resplendent on a hill in the Stromovka; it was rebuilt in a neo-Gothic style in the 19th century and today houses a library and a reading room of the Prague National Museum. Underneath the palace the remains of the so-called **Imperial Mill** can be found: this was a cutting mill used for working glass and precious stones. The palace was given to Emperor Rudolph II by the Estates. In the 19th century, one of Austria's most important paper factories was based here. At that time, the so-called **Rudolph Tunnel**, a tunnel of more than 100 m in length, was hewn through the Letná-massif to divert water from the Vltava into a large pond within the Royal Enclosure. The remains of this technical masterpiece can still be seen.

Pavilion in the gardens at the Castle's southern slope.

Petřín Hill with the Eiffel Tower in miniature.

In Prague's Cemetries

There are dozens of cemeteries in Prague, some of which are also rather interesting for visitors. Without doubt, the most important of these quiet but much visited graveyards is the **Czech National Cemetery on the Vyšehrad**. Many great figures in Czech national history have been laid to rest here: Poets such as Jan Neruda, Karel Hynek Mácha and Jaroslav Vrchlický; painters such as Max Švabinský, Alfons Mucha or Mikoláš Aleš; composers such as Antonín Dvořák, Zdeněk Fibich and Bedřich Smetana. Probably the most frequently visited graveyard is not on the Vyšehrad, however, but the **Old Jewish Cemetery** in the Jewish Quarter of Prague. Nonetheless, the **New Jewish Cemetery** in Prague Strašnice also attracts many visitors, indeed the most renowned grave of the city is here: the last resting-place of Franz Kafka (above left). The extended complex of the **Olšany Cemetery** [Olšanské hřbitovy] borders on the New Jewish Cemetery. Here, at the Olšany Cemetery, one of the largest cemeteries in Europe, lies a distinguished row of eminent personalities of the 19th century, for example the artists August Piepenhagen, Luděk Marold, Josef Lada and Josef Mánes, the philosopher Bernard Bolzano, or the poet Karel Jaromír Erben. More than a million people have been buried at Olšany; there are about 100,000 graves, some of which are of great art historical interest, among some 42 km of paths.

Unlike Olšany, which is frequently visited, the long-abandoned **Lesser Town Cemetery** is a kingdom fallen into a fairytale sleep amidst the thundering traffic. Here lie the Dušeks, Wolfgang Amadeus Mozart's hosts in Prague, the composers Wenzel Johann Tomaschek [also known as: Václav Jan Tomášek] and Jan Nepomuk Vitásek, as well as Vincenz Morstadt, draftsman and engraver of numerous Prague and Bohemian vedutas. A large graveyard can also be found in **Vinohrady**. Quite a few distinguished personalities of recent Czech cultural history are buried here, like Václav Havel, for example, builder of the Lucerna Palace and grandfather of the later president, or Jan Karafiát, author of Broučci (Little Beetles), a book every Czech child knows. In Smíchov is the **Malvazink churchyard**, where the author Jakub Arbes has been laid to rest. Somewhat on the outskirts, at **Břevnov cemetery**, we may find the grave of philosopher Jan Patočka. Here, too, lies buried the philanthropist Professor Alois Klar, who hailed from Úštěk in North Bohemia and was the founder of the first Home for the Blind in Prague.

Prague House Symbols

Long before the people of Prague identified their houses with numbers, they marked their dwellings by using so-called house symbols, whose imagery is usually linked in some way or another to the history of the house itself, or to the trade that was practiced within its walls (like bells, cans, rings, goblets, keys, etc.). The house symbols (animals, especially lions and lambs, donkeys and bears, carps and snakes, furthermore candles, shoes, violins, wheels, hearts, angels, stars, grapes, horseshoes and many others) were modeled in plaster, chiseled in stone, painted on the façade or forged in iron. Accordingly, the buildings were given such melodious names as "At the Blue Snake" or "At the Golden Swan".

How skilled the old masters were, and how poetic were the proud house owners! Many symbols differ only in a few details, and several are repeated, as the individual districts of the modern city were independent from each well into the 18th century.

In 1770, a consecutive chronological numbering of buildings was introduced with the so-called conscription numbers (white numbers on a red background); the present numbering system (white numbers on a blue background) has prevailed since 1878. This sounded the death knell for the tradition of house symbols! Along the Royal Path, however, in the **Canvas Makers' Lane** [Celetná], or up steep **Neruda Lane** in the Lesser Town, for example, many of these small works of art have been lovingly preserved and survive into our day. It is well worth raising your head and looking out for them!

On 20ᵗʰ Century Architecture

Figurehead on Čech-Bridge (Art Nouveau).

The television tower in Žižkov (Futurism). ▶

Villa Müller (Functionalism).

Year after year, visitors flock to Prague to see a historical city kept largely intact and soak up the air of past centuries. But the so-called modern spirit has also left its mark on the face of the city – with both masterly buildings and ghastly ones, with buildings of timeless beauty as well as those bound to the fashion of their day.

The blossoming of Art Nouveau at the beginning of the 20ᵗʰ century chimed perfectly with the national romanticistic folklore. After the First World War came the triumph of Cubism, which was displaced by Functionalism during the 1920s when it appeared as a kind of avant-garde movement. The architecture of Josip Plečnik strikes a particular note; called to the city on the Vltava from his home in Slovakia, among other projects he modernised Prague Castle in the spirit of the new republic.

These developments were brought more or less to a standstill by the Second World War and the country's subsequent absorbtion into the communist sphere of control. The cityscape suffered serious damage as a result of entire suburbs of prefabricated panel buildings and gigantic traffic projects. One of the largest building projects of the century was the underground railway, which was pushed forward from the 1970s onward. The city expressway, the "magistrála", cuts a brutal swath through the city centre – an exercise in car-friendly traffic policy, for which the idyllic municipal park and the elegant square in front of the main railway station were sacrificed. Only the Velvet Revolution of 1989 eventually brought new options, although admittedly accompanied by great risks. Would the incomparable cityscape suffer further damage from the unchecked boom in investment? The protection of historical monuments is often no match for the astronomical sums offered by international investors.

The most important architectural achievements of the 20th century can only be illustrated by means of a select few examples. In the city centre: the renovation of **Prague Castle** dating from the twenties, the rebuilding of **Prague central station** by Josef Fanta (1901–1909), the **Svatopluk-Čech-Bridge** (1905–1908), the Cubist department store **"House of the Black Madonna"** by Josef Gočár (1911–1912), the Art Nouveau **Municipal House** adjacent to the Powder Tower by Osvald Polívka and Antonín Balšánek (1905–1912), the palace of the insurance company **Riunione Adriatica di Sicurtà** on Jungmannova Street (1922–1925), and of course the splendid edifices on Wenceslas Square, among them, the **Peterka department store** by Jan Kotěra (1899–1900), the Secessionist **Grandhotel Evropa** by Bendlmayer, Letzl and Hypšman (1903–1905), the **Koruna Palace** by Antonín Pfeiffer (1911–1914), the **department stores Lindt** (1925–1927) **and Baťa** (1927–1929) by Ludvík Kysela, and last but not least the **Hotel Juliš** by Pavel Janák (1928–1933).

One of Prague's first reinforced concrete skeleton constructions is on Vodičkova Street – the **Lucerna Palace** built by Václav Havel, grandfather of the later President of the same name; close by is the striking Art Nouveau palace **"U Nováků"** by Osvald Polívka. The Functionalist-romantic **Mánes House** by Otakar Novotný (1927–1930) salutes the observer from the Masaryk embankment [Masarykovo nábřeží] on the Vltava. The annexe to the National Theatre, the **Nová Scéna** built of Cuban glass elements, is crudely disturbing. Just as controversial is the **Dancing House** [Tančící dům] (Ginger and Fred) on the Vltava quay, a prestigious building designed by Frank O. Gehry.

On the outskirts, striking examples of modern architecture are even more frequent than in the centre: the **Žižka monument** by Jan Zázvorka at Vítkov Hill (1926–1932), the **Municipal Waterworks** by Antonín Engel in Podolí (1923–1928), the **Film studios** and restaurant by Max Urban in Barrandov (1929–1934), the **Baba Villas** in Dejvice (1928–1934), **Villa Müller** by Adolf Loos in Střešovice (1928–1930), the **Prague Exhibition Palace** by Oldřich Tyl and Josef Fuchs in Holešovice (1924–1928), **St Wenceslas' Church** by Josef Gočár in Vršovice (1928–1933), or the **terminal of the old airport** by Adolf Benš und Kamil Roškot (1934–1935) are just a few.

On Czech Beer

Czech "pivo" enjoys an excellent reputation world-wide. The famous "Pilsner Urquell" [Plzeňský Prazdroj] and the "Original Budweiser" are of course on tap all over the country, but the lesser known brands can hold their own too: Krušovice's dark beer, the smooth "Bernard" from the family Humpolec brewery, "Starobrno" by the "First Brno Joint Stock Brewery" established in 1872, or "Regent", a brew from Třebon by probably the oldest brewery in the country. Of course, the heirs to the throne in the world famous beer cities are not to be forgotten either: As well as "Urquell", the popular 10-degree "Gambrinus" hails from Plzeň, and the south Bohemian city of České Budějovice is home not only to "Original Budweiser", but also to the quaffable "Samson".

Prague of course brews its own excellent beer as it has done for almost a thousand years. The Prague Joint Stock Brewery in Smíchov has produced the mild 10-degree "Staropramen" ("Old Spring") since 1871, considered by many Prague residents to be the pinnacle of the brewer's art.

The competition begs to differ, of course! "U Fleků" for example, is the legendary and

quaint Prague brewery restaurant, where traditional beer coziness is taken seriously. This tavern has been selling the unsurpassable Flek beer since the 15th century, although only under the current name since 1762: that was when a certain Jakub Flekovský took over the pub and paved the way for its success. It is a dark beer with a caramel flavour, made from Prague water, hops from Žatec and four different kinds of malt; 6,000 hectolitres of Flek are tapped a year, and the memory of the delicious brew and the noisy but incomparable atmosphere is enough to make many beer connoisseurs smack their lips, even years later.

The clock at the beer-restaurant "U Fleků".

"U Fleků" is not the only pub well worth a visit; plenty of others also attract beer-lovers with their unique charm. The beer-restaurant "U Kalicha" has been made famous by Jaroslav Hašek's novel *The Good Soldier Švejk*. A visit to this pub is on the to-do-list of any hearty beer drinker. The 14th century St Thomas' Cellar in Thomas' Lane [Tomášská] in the Lesser Town is still awaiting rebirth; until 1953, a home-brewed dark ale was served from its vaults.

Beer-lovers with a taste for exploration would do well to make an expedition towards the outskirts, to Žižkov, for example, a district popular among night revellers and home to numerous original beer pubs.

The Joint-Stock Brewery works in Pilsen.

The Defenestrations of Prague

Contemporary engraving of the Second Defenestration of Prague (1618).

It is an old Czech custom, say the mockers, to thrust political opponents into the depths below any suitable window at the first opportunity. Indeed – there have been a few cases of such

ungentle treatment in the dim and distant past. Three defenestrations, in the narrower sense of the word, hold a particular position in the collective memory of Prague residents. First of all, there is the so-called First Defenestration of Prague, where radical Hussites threw a judge and several councillors out of a window in the City Hall of the New Town of Prague. Eleven lives were lost in this violent incident. The defenestration on 23rd of May 1618 also comes to mind, when Bohemian Protestants dispatched two imperial councillors and their secretary from the Bohemian Chancellery. The three unfortunates got off rather luckily from the ordeal – they made a soft landing, so the story goes, on a dung heap. But the defenestration lit the torch for the outbreak of the Thirty Years' War, which laid large parts of the empire waste and decimated its population.

The death of Jan Masaryk, son of the republic's first president, is often referred to as the Third Defenestration of Prague. In 1948, he fell to his death from a window at Černín Palace, in mysterious circumstances. His demise is thought to be linked to a political conspiracy.

Prague Spring '68

After 1948, Czechoslovakia was an orthodox Socialist People's Republic at the side of the Soviet Union. Then, in the sixties, a distinct political thaw set in. The leader of the communist party, Alexandr Dubček, introduced reforms in 1968 which nurtured hopes of a free and independent development in the country. As the protecting power, the USSR could not stand by and watch. On 21ˢᵗ August 1968, armed forces of the Warsaw Pact marched into Czechoslovakia and put a forcible end to the era of reform. In the following years of "normalisation", the Soviet ally took a hard line with Czechoslovakia, the reforms were reversed and the political leadership of the so-called Prague Spring removed from power. As a result, a large number of intellectuals, writers and artists left the country or went into hiding. The much-longed-for change took place only in 1989 with the "Velvet Revolution".

Wenceslas Square has been the scene of important political demonstrations.

1968: Young demonstrators protest against the invasion by forces of the Warsaw Pact.

The "Velvet Revolution"

In the summer of 1989, thousands of Germans from the GDR fled to the West German embassy to force the authorities to grant them refuge in the FRG. The streets in the city were full of parked "Trabbis" and Wartburgs, cars of East German production. Finally, the West German Minister for Foreign Affairs, Hans-Dietrich Genscher, announced to the refugees holding out in the provisional emergency lodgings that they had been granted permission to leave their country. Then, on the 9th November came the memorable day when the Berlin Wall came down. Czechoslovakia was in a state of – then – quiet suspense. On the 17th November 1989 the situation escalated. A shaken police force attacked students who had demonstrated against the hated regime. One of the last bulwarks of European Communism began to sway. Soon afterwards, the demonstrating students were joined by actors and artists, academics and workers. The streets filled up, intimidated law enforcement units anxiously watched the swelling national movement. Hundreds of thousands of Prague residents gathered at Wenceslas

Summer 1989: Citizens of East Germany escape to the Embassy of West Germany.

Square. With bunches of keys, the crowds finally jangled the end of the totalitarian People's Republic; the Communist leadership had no choice but to transfer power into the hands of the former dissidents. A citizen's forum was established, to pool the strengths of the opposition. On the 24th November, the Communist government resigned and on the 25th November around 750,000 Czechs gathered on the Letná fields to reinforce their demands for political reforms. A general strike was followed by victory, triumph – and the protest turned into exuberant celebrations.

The men of the hour were Alexandr Dubček, the hero of the Prague Spring in 1968, and Václav Havel, the renowned dramatist who had been released from state prison only a few months before. It was not long before the walls read: Havel na Hrad – Havel to the Castle!

These turbulent days are today known as the "Velvet Revolution", which makes it easy to forget that there were beatings and violence, and that nobody was certain whether the officials would resort to firearms to quell the uprising. The fear and the anxiety are also forgotten. Only the happiness is remembered, when the nightmare that had lasted for decades finally came to an end and the future could begin.

November 1989: Václav Havel and Alexandr Dubček speak to the masses at the peaceful protests on Wenceslas Square.

Prague and Music

Bohemian musicians.

Prague has one of the longest-standing traditions as a centre of music in Europe, and the Czechs have always been one of the most influential nations of music in the world! There is singing, music and playing everywhere, in churches, palaces and concert halls. Antonín Dvořák, Zdeněk Fibich and Bedřich Smetana lived in Prague, Josef Mysliveček, "the divine Bohemian" (Il divino Boemo) was born here, Leoš Janáček and Bohumil Martinů celebrated their greatest successes here.

Generations of Bohemian musicians were educated at the renowned **Prague Conservatory**; Czech masters went out into the world from here. But foreign maestros (such as Antonio Vivaldi, Wolfgang Amadeus Mozart, Ludwig van Beethoven, Carl Maria von Weber, Niccolò Paganini, Franz Liszt, Frédéric Chopin or Peter Illyich Tchaikovsky), were also al-

Billboards advertise concerts all over the city.

ways glad to perform in Prague as they were certain to meet with a knowledgable and music-loving audience.

The well-established "Prague Spring" [Pražské jaro] festival has an excellent reputation, and has recently been complemented by a second festival – the "Prague Autumn" [Pražský podzim].

Among the most important venues for music are the **National Theatre**, the **Estates' Theatre**, the **State Opera** – the former New German Theatre –, the **House of Artists** [Rudolfinum], the **Smetana Hall** in the Municipal House [Obecní dům], the **House "At the Stone Bell"** on the Old Town Square [U Kamen- ného zvonu], and numerous churches where concerts are held. The **Villa Amerika**, created by the Baroque master builder Kilian Ignaz Dientzenhofer in the New Town, houses an Antonín Dvořák Museum that is well worth seeing. Not far from Charles Bridge, is the **Smetana Museum** at the Novotný Footbridge [Novotného lávka]. Opened in 1936, it displays mem- orabilia from Bedřich Smetana's life: manuscripts, photographs, fragments of his diary, correspondence, the programme of his first concert in Prague, a silver conductor's baton, his oldest preserved composition – the 1832 *Gallop in D-Major* – as well as the piano on which he composed the operas *Libuše* and *The Bartered Bride*. Lovers of old instruments should not miss the **Czech Music Museum**, opened in 2004.

Czech jazz virtuoso at Charles Bridge.

Statue of Antonín Dvo- řák in front of the Rudol- finum.

The Czech Philharmonic Orchestra, the na- tion's most important ensemble, performs in all the great concert halls of the world. Unknown beyond on the banks of the Vltava, however, is the Secessionist "Hlahol", where traditional na- tional choral singing is practiced and lovingly preserved. Many tourists of course come to visit the Mozart sites in Prague, first and foremost **Villa Bertramka** in Smíchov, where chamber concerts resound on warm summer evenings. Prague also has a lot to offer to jazz lovers, such as a **jazz cruise** on the Vltava or the **Jazz- club Reduta**, where even Bill Clinton once reached for his saxophone. Dixieland and Swing music can often be heard on Charles Bridge and other streets and squares. Even zither-players let their music sound under the open sky, and on greeting the musician, you can suddenly find yourself engaged in con- versation with an authority on old stringed instruments.

Mozart and Prague

An impression of Mozart's time: A gallant couple at the Fürstenberg Garden.

After Salzburg and Vienna, Prague is the third city inseparably bound up with the name of Mozart. The composer celebrated his greatest triumphs in the Bohemian capital; here even the ballad-mongers and street urchins understood the arias of his operas, while the audience in the imperial city of Vienna turned up their illustrious noses at them. All in all, Kapellmeister Wolfgang Amadeus Mozart paid five visits to the capital on the Vltava, three of which were longer stays: in January and February 1787 he made a cheerful trip to Prague to introduce himself to an audience which had been enthused by his opera *Le nozze di Figaro* (The Marriage of Figaro); he came again in au-

Estates' Theatre in the Old Town of Prague.

tumn 1787, when he attended the première of his opera *Don Giovanni* in the Estates' Theatre; he returned for a final time in 1791, when he was commissioned to compose an opera on the occasion of the coronation of Leopold II as king of Bohemia (*La clemenza di Tito*). Among Mozart's friends in Prague were Czech the composer František Dušek and his wife, the singer Josepha Dušková. The couple owned what today is without doubt the most popular site connected with Mozart in Prague, namely Villa Bertramka, a former

country estate in the Smíchov district. Mozart was repeatedly a guest there and created some of his most beautiful pieces of music in this idyllic rural retreat. His appreciative comment that "My people in Prague understand me" has gone down in the annals of the city.

Villa Bertramka in Smíchov.

Mozart, Don Giovanni, Introduktion

Mozart, Don Giovanni, 2. Aufzug

Elvira

E mio ma ri to!

St Nepomuk, the Bridge Guardian

In all of Bohemia, throughout Europe, indeed, across the world we encounter him as a silent guardian on bridges and passageways. Whether it be in the wooded valleys of Carinthia in Austria, in the villages of Tuscany or in the cities of South America – Nepomuk watches over the seal of confession in countless churches and his likeness is venerated. And most of the time, he is portrayed together with a part of Prague – the Charles Bridge. It was there that in 1393, pious John from the Bohemian town of Nepomuk ended his life a martyr, when King Wenceslas IV had him thrown from the stone bridge spanning the Vltava into the floods below. The legend goes that John of Nepomuk chose not to divulge the secrets of pious Queen Sophie's confession as the cruel king demanded, thus forfeiting his life.

His afterlife as one of the most popular saints began with signs and wonders in Prague. Legend reports: *"Nobody knew where the corpse lay. But the water level, which, in spring, had been high, became conspicuously lower, so that the plain drying up of the River Vltava was considered to be sent by God. The corpse became visible. However, the king, in his scorn, would not have it lifted. Suddenly, on the night of the 17th to the 18th of April, wonderful lights shone on the corpse. Attracted by the glow, everybody gathered to see the holy corpse. The canons raised him without a thought for the king's rage and carried him into the Chapel of the Holy Cross, to stay there until a suitable tomb was prepared for the saint in the cathedral [...]. In 1719, the tomb was opened;*

the bones were found to be in good condition and the tongue was not decayed at all, only dried up. During an examination, it turned a living dark red colour and shape, an effect which intensified into a crimson colour over the span of two hours. Thus did God glorify this part of the body which, after having dutifully remained silent, now spoke out all the louder and even more emphatically through its unscathed condition."

In 1683, almost 300 years after his martyrdom, the bronze statue of St Nepomuk by Johann Brokoff was put up on Charles Bridge.

The cult of St Nepomuk reached its climax in the Baroque era and especially after his canonisation in 1721; at that time, the saint's magnificent silver tomb in St Vitus' Cathedral was created. As a result, believers flocked to Prague on the feast day of St John of Nepomuk, the 16th of May, to commemorate the martyr with prayers and pious celebrations at Charles Bridge.

John of Nepomuk's dead body on the Vltava (Franz Xaver Karl Palko, National Galery). ▼

The Golem

According to legend, the Golem was an artificial being made of clay. The Prague Rabbi Loew created him in a secret ritual to protect the Jews of Prague. When he came to life, he was named Josef and the Rabbi gave him the clothes of a Shammes. Though the Golem could not speak, he obediently fulfilled the tasks assigned to him with zeal and devotion. Under certain circumstances however, the zealous and good-natured servant could turn into a dangerous monster, rampaging through the Jewish Quarter and wreaking havoc.

Various artistic renderings of the Golem.

On one such occasion, stamping through the streets of the Ghetto, he forfeited his life: the esteemed Rabbi Loew transformed him back into a lump of clay in the attic of the Old-New Synagogue. Ever since, it has been forbidden for anyone to enter the attic of the synagogue on pain of severe punishment.

There is a variety of different Golem legends; nor is the figure of the Golem exclusive to Prague. However, a widely-read novel by the Prague writer Gustav Meyrink entitled *The Golem* has contributed hugely to the popularisation of the figure and thus linked it to the city of Prague. Literary adaptations, films, artistic creations as well as the general interest in Jewish Prague and the esoteric doctrines of cabbala – have made the Golem a central figure of the Prague Jewish Quarter.

Franz Kafka and Prague

Kafka's place of work: Workers' Accident Insurance Company for the Kingdom of Bohemia in Prague.

Kafka's world: Old Town Square.

"... a book must be the axe to break the frozen sea within us. That's what I believe."

Franz Kafka has become a synonym for turn-of-the-century Prague like no other. Visitors come by the thousands to trace his footsteps on the banks of the Vltava. Ironically, the German Jewish writer wanted all his life to get away from his birthplace, of which he said: "Prague won't let go […] We would have to set fire to two places, Vyšehrad and Prague Castle, and then it might be possible for us to get away."

Franz Kafka was born in 1883 on the outskirts of the then still existing Prague ghetto. After his studies at the German University of Prague, Kafka worked as a lawyer in the Work-

ers' Accident Insurance Company of the Kingdom of Bohemia in Prague. The author's private life was strongly influenced by his father whom he felt to be overpowering, and his own inability to start a family of his own: He twice broke off his engagement to Felice Bauer from Berlin because he sought solitude as a writer. Neither did his love for the married Czech journalist Milena Jesenská lead to a shared future.

Kafka as a grammar school student.

Franz Kafka's first prose volume *Meditation* was published in a small edition in 1912. Kafka soon became an author of distinction in noted literary circles. Yet he would not live to see his rise as a writer of international acclaim: tuberculosis led to Kafka's early retirement and, ultimately, his premature death. He died in a sanatorium near Vienna in 1924.

His friend Max Brod prevented the loss of his literary estate, the author's will having stipulated that it should be destroyed, and published Kafka's works after the artist's death. Since then, the posthumously published novels have ranked among the most outstanding creations of the 20th Century, indeed of German literature in general. Kafka's works are read worldwide, triggering a constant flow of interpretations, of which it has long since been impossible to keep an overview. Among his most important works are the novels *The Trial* and *The Castle*, the short stories *The Judgement* and *The Metamorphosis*, as well as diaries and letters (to his sister Ottla, to his fiancée Felice, to his lover Milena) and the key biographical document *Letter to Father*.

Kafka at the age of 31.

"Kafka was Prague and Prague was Kafka. Never was Prague so perfect, so typical of herself as she was during Kafka's lifetime, and never will she be so again. And we, his friends, we knew that this Prague subtly pervaded all his writing."

(Johannes Urzidil)

Kafka with his fiancée Felice Bauer.

45

10 x Prague Literature

Bohumil Hrabal (1914–1997), born in Brno, spent his childhood mostly in the central Bohemian town of Nymburk and became a student of law in Prague. After the Communist coup, Hrabal worked, among other odd jobs, as a blast furnace worker in Kladno and as a scene shifter in a theatre in Prague. From 1962 on he devoted himself exclusively to literary work, while his earlier experiences provided the backdrop for his largely autobiographical prose. He did not submit to the socialist doctrine and accordingly got caught in the crosshairs of censorship several times, often only being able to publish his works in the so-called "Samisdat" or in exiled publishing houses; despite this, however, Hrabal succeeded in becoming one of the most important postwar authors in Czechoslovakia (next to Milan Kundera and Jaroslav Seifert). His writings, centring on the fate of the ordinary man and pervaded by his earthy humour, are read worldwide by an audience of millions, yet it is only since 1989 that they can be published in his homeland unmutilated. By then, Hrabal had long since become a famous author, highly respected in the literary world. After the "Velvet Revolution", the writer, living in rural seclusion, became something akin to a father of the gods on the Olympus of Czech literature. A fall from a hospital window sill, onto which he had climbed to feed pigeons, ended his life in 1997, after it had spanned almost the entire 20th century.

Important works:
Dancing Lessons for the Advanced in Age (1964)
The Palaverers (1964)
Cutting it Short (1976)
Snowdrop Festivities (1980)
I Served the King of England (1982)

Franz Werfel (1890–1945) was born in Prague. The novelist, storyteller and lyric poet Franz Werfel came from a wealthy Jewish factory owner's family. Werfel started out by composing poems and writing dramas while he was still a pupil at the New Town German Grammar School, and by 1910, the Expressionist lyricist was already well-known and considered the focal point of the Prague "Arco"-Circle. In 1912 he became an editor for Kurt Wolff Publishers in Leipzig, for whom he launched the avant-garde edition *Der Jüngste Tag* (Judgement Day). After his service in the First World War he moved to Vienna, where he married Gustav Mahler's widow. He was forced to leave Vienna in 1938 and went into exile. After a series of detours he reached the USA and there succumbed to a heart condition after the end of the war. At the core of his literary and essayist works are issues of faith as well as the battle against a disintegration of values. His greatest popular successes were his novels *Embezzled Heaven* (1939) and *The Song of Bernadette* (1941).

Other important works:
   Verdi. A Novel of the Opera (1924)
   The Forty Days of Musa Dagh (1933)
   The Star of the Unborn (1946)

Jan Neruda (1834–1891), born in the Lesser Town in Prague, was brought up in poor circumstances. His father worked in a barracks' kitchen and his mother was a maid. He was forced to give up his promising studies of law and philosophy due to a lack of funds. After 1856, Neruda worked as a local reporter, and soon his first poetry and prose emerged. In his writings the Naturalistic author meditates on the fate of the Czech nation.

His influential prose work *Arabesques* was published in 1864, followed in 1878 by the *Prague Tales from the Little Quarter*, still popular today, in which he immortalises the lot of the many characters and ordinary people of

this part of town in an apparently idyllic and often ironic manner.

Other important works:
Cemetery Flowers (1858)
Cosmic Songs (1878)
Ballads and Romances (1883)

Johannes Urzidil (1896–1970), born in Prague, studied German and Slavonic philology and art history at Charles University. In the 1920s he was the press adviser for the German embassy in Prague and frequented the literary circles of his home city (and thus rubbed shoulders with Franz Werfel, Franz Kafka, Max Brod and others). Urzidil made a name for himself even before the Second World War as not only an Expressionist lyric poet, but also as a cultural historian and journalist. In 1939 he emigrated via Italy to England and continued on to the United States in 1941. After the war, Urzidil won literary acclaim for his narrative works. In 1964 he was awarded the Great Austrian State Prize for European Literature.

Important works:
The Fall of the Damned (1919)
Goethe in Bohemia (1932)
The Lost Beloved (1956)
The Prague Triptych (1960)

Leo Perutz (1882–1957) came from a Jewish merchant's family in Prague. He moved to Vienna with his family when he was 17. After training in the insurance business he was employed as an actuary for several years.

His first work *The Third Bullet* (1915) was a success to which he could immediately tie in with his next novel *From Nine to Nine* (1918). Friedrich Torberg called Perutz "Franz Kafka's misstep with Agatha Christie." In the early twenties, Perutz gave up his middle-class job in favour for a life as a professional writer. The tide turned however after the National Socialists came to power: his writings were banned in Germany, in 1938 Perutz was forced to leave Austria and emigrated, initially to

Israel. For a long time his work disappeared into oblivion, since the 1990s, however, it has experienced a remarkable renaissance.

Other important works:
  Little Apple (1928)
  The Swedish Cavalier (1936)
  By Night under the Stone Bridge (1953)

Egon Erwin Kisch (1885–1948), born in Prague, came from a reputable Jewish draper's family. He worked as a local reporter and acquired an intimate knowledge of life in Prague. In *Aus Prager Gassen und Nächten* (*From the Lanes and Nights of Prague*), a work published in 1912, he principally portrays the socially isolated environment of brothels and public houses. His only novel *Der Mädchenhirt* (*The Shepherd of Girls*) (1914) is similarly set in this demi-monde. After the First World War, Kisch became involved with the Communist party and worked for the journals *Weltbühne* (*World Stage*) and *Rote Fahne* (*Red Flag*) in Berlin. Kisch attained great popularity with his volume *Der Rasende Reporter* (1924) (*The Racing Reporter*), a collection of reports whose title was to become his nickname. As a communist he was forced to go into exile in 1933, which took him via France, Great Britain and Spain to Mexico. Shortly after the end of the war he returned to Prague where he died soon after.

Other important works:
  The Case of Colonel Redl (1924)
  Rush Through Time (1926)
  Discoveries in Mexico (1945)

Gustav Meyrink (1868–1932) was born in Vienna and came to Prague at the age of 17. Later renowned as a novelist and author of short stories, he founded a Christian banking house but his eccentric lifestyle brought him opposition, especially in middle-class circles. After three months of imprisonment, Meyrink's existence in Prague was ruined and he was compelled to leave the city in 1903. After short spells in Vienna and Munich he settled

down in Starnberg, where he conceived his novel *The Golem* (1915), which was to make him internationally famous. Gustav Meyrink is counted among the founders of fantastical literature. Characteristic of his works are mystical influences and a tendency towards occultism.

Other important works:
Des deutschen Spießers Wunderhorn (The German Philistine's Horn) (1913)
The Green Face (1917)
Walpurgisnacht (Walpurgis Night) (1917)
The White Dominican (1921)

Jaroslav Hašek (1883–1923) was born in Prague. After studying at a commercial college and a brief stint as a bank employee, he led the life of a vagrant and bohemian from 1902. He travelled the entire Austrian-Hungarian Empire and Europe. Hašek sympathised with the then modern anarchist movement, edited their periodicals and wrote incendiary features and humorous sketches. To ridicule the parliamentary elections, he founded the "Party of Moderate Progress within the Limits of Law". At the outbreak of the First World War, he went to the Russian front and eventually joined the Czechoslovakian Legion by a somewhat roundabout route. After the October Revolution he worked as a journalist for the Red Army. He returned to Prague in 1920, withdrew from politics, made his appearance in the cabaret "Červená sedma" (Red Seven) and continued to dedicate himself to the composition of his novel *The Good Soldier Švejk* (1912–1923), which was initially rejected by contemporary critics as being vulgar and inartistic. Only after the novel was translated into German did it become a huge success and gain access to world literature as the most significant Czech work.

Important works:
The Good Soldier Švejk and Other Peculiar Anecdotes (1912)
The Good Soldier Švejk in Captivity (1917)
The Fateful Adventures of the Good Soldier Švejk during the World War (1921–23)

Karel Čapek (1890–1938), son of a country doctor from Malé Svatoňovice, worked as a journalist after 1917. He was director and dramatic adviser at the theatre in the district of Vinohrady. In the years 1925–1933, he was the first chairman of the Czechoslovakian PEN club. Čapek actively participated in the political and artistic life of Prague and eventually became the major representative of cultural life of Czechoslovakia. His works have been translated into all world languages. In the thirties, Čapek engaged himself in the battle against the growing influence of National Socialism. He created plays such as *The White Disease* (1937) (also translated as *Power and Glory*) and *The Mother* (1938), as well as the novel *War with the Newts* (1936). Typical of Čapek's work is his search for a meaning in existence and for more profound knowledge.

Other important works:
   Rossum's Universal Robots (1920)
   The Absolute at Large (1922)
   Krakatit (1924)

Rainer Maria Rilke (1875–1926) was born in Prague. After graduating from a military school, the lyric poet and storyteller studied art, literature, and legal history in Prague, Berlin, and elsewhere. His Bohemian homeland is often at the heart of his early poems and stories. Unlike Franz Kafka, Rilke left Prague in his younger years. He settled down in Worpswede with the sculptress Clara Westhoff, until, after a marital break-up in 1902, he began to lead an unstable life marked by a great deal of travel. His work reflects, among other things, his visits to Paris, where he was Auguste Rodin's secretary in 1905/1906, and Duino on the Mediterranean with Princess Marie of Thurn and Taxis.

Important works:
   Larenopfer (Lares' Sacrifice) (1896)
   Two Prague Stories (1898)
   The Book of Images (1902)
   The Notebook of Malte Laurids Brigge (1910)
   Duino Elegies (1922)

The Castle District
[Hradčany]

Prague Castle Guards in their flattering uniforms.

A Visit to the Castle District
[Hradčany]

The old imperial stronghold of Prague Castle and the adjoining Castle District [Hradčany] are situated on an elongated rocky hill on the left bank of the River Vltava. The name of the district is derived from the Czech term "hrad", meaning castle. Besides the extensive castle itself, it also comprises the impressive Strahov Monastery, once on the periphery of the castle, as well as the Royal Gardens and the Belvedere summer residence. The most influential noblemen of the country built their palaces in this fashionable quarter, in close proximity to the king. The families of Martinic, Černín, Lobkowicz, Rosenberg, Schwarzenberg and Dietrichstein lived there, at eye-level with his Imperial Majesty. Building plots in the Castle District became scarce in the 17th century, so that the nobility was eventually forced to move towards the foot of the hill, to the Lesser Town [Malá Strana].

The origins of Prague Castle stretch back to the 9th century, when the first Christian Přemyslid ruler, Bořivoj I, moved his capital from Levý Hradec to the banks of the Vltava (875). A few years later in 890, a stone church consecrated to the Blessed Virgin Mary was built at the wooden castle, protected by ramparts and a moat. Bořivoj's son, Vratislav I, had a second church built on the site now occupied by St George's Basilica. After the establishment of a diocese of Prague during the reign of Boleslav II in 973, the castle also served as the seat of the bishops.

Emperor Charles IV of Luxembourg rebuilt the castle which had fallen into ruin after the time of Přemysl Otakar II, and made it the focal point of the Holy Roman Empire. When Prague was eleveated to an archdiocese in 1344, he ordered a Gothic cathedral to be built – St Vitus' Cathedral.

After several years of decline following the Hussite wars, it was the Jagiellonian kings who brought back a glittering and bustling lifestyle to the castle at the end of the 15th century. The Royal Court in the Old Town, although comfortable, was undefended and they no longer felt secure there during the uprisings of 1483.

The Habsburg dynasty, in power after 1526, surrounded the estate with gardens, built the splendid Belvedere summer residence and transformed the inhospitable fortress into a luxurious palace.

The fire that devastated the Lesser Town and the Castle District in 1541 breached the medieval character of the city. However, the necessary building and rebuilding which resulted helped the Renaissance, which was already on the rise elsewhere, to make the final breakthrough into the Castle District.

The castle blossomed once more under Rudolph II, the legendary Habsburg emperor, who made Prague the cultural and political focal point of the Holy Roman Empire for one last time. The collector, patron of the arts and builder had a series of extensions built (the north wing with the Spanish Hall and the Rudolph Gallery, for example) and had a deer enclosure established in the moat behind the Castle as well as the stone Lion Courtyard, a pheasantery, a fishpond and a summer riding school.

In 1618, the Estates' Rebellion and the Thirty Years' War were sparked by the so-called Second Defenestration of Prague, which took place at Prague Castle. The imperial governors Jaroslav Martinic and Vilém of Slavata were thrown out of a window in the Bohemian Chancellery, along with the secretary Phillipus Fabricius. In the course of the ensuing Thirty Years' War the castle was occupied by Saxon and Swedish armies. Invaluable artistic treasures from the Rudolphine collections were lost or destroyed.

Emperor Rudolph II elevated the whole area to a Royal District and, 150 years later, Maria Theresa declared the Castle District to be the fourth city of Prague.

The castle was besieged and damaged several times during the 18th century as a result of Maria Theresia's War of Austrian Succession: by a Franco-Saxon army in 1741 and by the Prussians in both 1744 and 1757. However, the castle also witnessed boisterous celebrations, such as the canonisation of John of Nepomuk in 1721, the festivities at the coronation of Charles VI as King of Bohe-

The Castle District as seen from Petřín Hill.

Strahov Monastery behind townhouses of the Lesser Town.

mia in 1711, and, after bitter battles over the succession, the enthronement of Maria Theresia in 1743, who was ultimately victorious and acclaimed as empress.

During the reign of her son Joseph II, not only were the last remains of the collections of Rudolph II auctioned, but extensive damage was also done to the castle through the thoughtless billeting of soldiers in places like the Royal Summer Residence, St George's Convent, the Royal Riding School and the large Ballroom Hall. An Emperor was to live in the castle for one last time, however, even though it had long been sunk in fairytale slumber: the unfortunate Emperor Ferdinand I (known as "the Kind-Hearted"), who, following his abdication in 1848, found a permanent place of rest far away from the court of Vienna in the seclusion of Prague Castle.

After 1918, the president of the fledgling Czechoslovakian Republic, Tomáš Garrigue Masaryk, held office at the castle, the seat of the highest authority in the country. Prague Castle underwent extensive renovations to suit the requirements of the Presidential Chancellery. In 1920, the Slovene architect Josip Plečnik began remodelling the Castle Gardens and Courtyards as well as the presidential residence and function rooms. The reconstruction and research work continues to this day.

Since 1993, the president of the Czech Republic has officiated from Prague Castle.

Strahov Monastery   1

[Strahovský klášter, Strahovské nádvoří 1]   Ⓣ 22 POHOŘELEC

In 1148, King Vladislav I had a monastery built on the foothills of Petřín Hill at the gates of the town. Premonstratensian monks from Steinfeld in the Eifel region moved into the originally wooden monastery. In the course of the centuries, after numerous alterations and extensions, the Premonstratensian monastery developed into one of the most important spiritual centres and one of the richest abbeys in the country, into a place of arts and sciences.

In the 13th century, a fire reduced the monastery to ash and rubble; in the course of the succeeding centuries, Strahov was repeatedly battererd by the violent tides of events (Hussite wars, the Thirty Years' War, the Prussian siege).

From Pohořelec, the "Scene of Fire", a ramp-like driveway leads up to the monastery entrance. To the right of the archway, parts of the so-called Hunger Wall, erected during the reign of Charles IV, can be seen. It owes its name to a famine: it is said that its construction allowed the people of Prague to earn their daily bread in this destitute time.

A statue of St Norbert made by Johann Anton Quittainer in 1755 overlooks the gate, additionally adorned with a coat of arms.

Resting on an ionic pillar between old trees in the courtyard behind the monastery is another statue of St Norbert. As the founder of the order, he receives special reverence at Strahov.

Two places of worship can be visited in the courtyard: to the left of the entrance is the parish church and burial **chapel of St Roch**, which was donated by Emperor Rudolph II as a gesture of gratitude for the salvation from the plague at the beginning of the 17th century. Its outlines are late Gothic, but the entrance with the winged angel's head points towards the approaching Renaissance. Today the church is deconsecrated and houses a gallery. More impressive by far is the magnificent **Church of the As-**

Gateway to Strahov Monastery.

Strahov: Statue of St Norbert of
Prémontre in the monastery courtyard.

ognize my Pappenheimers". One of
many further treasures in the church
interior is the great organ on which
Mozart is believed to have played in
1787.

Adjacent to the church is the new **library building** erected from 1782 to 1784 following the plans of Ignaz Palliardi. The interesting classicist façade is a lasting testimony of the enlightened spirit of Freemason Abbot Wenzel Mayer. The medallion in the tympanum by Ignaz Michael Platzer shows Emperor Joseph II, who sanctioned the construction of the building even though he had numerous other monasteries dissolved.

Visitors are prohibited from the 50,000 volume Philosophical Library on conservation grounds. The marvellous ceiling fresco, which depicts human intellectual history in lucid colours, can thus not be admired at close range. This is indeed a unique pictorial cycle created in 1794 in the space of just six months by the Baroque master Franz Anton Maulbertsch, at the age of 70.

The walnut furniture is originally from the south Moravian monastery of Louka near Znojmo, which was dissolved in the Josephine Reforms. The white monks of Strahov however were spared from the Emperor's reformist zeal. It was not until 1953 that the canons had to leave the monastery, ceding it to the atheist government for a few decades. Since then, however, the members of the order have returned to Strahov.

sumption, an originally Romanesque basilica which was remodelled to suit Baroque tastes by Anselmo Lurago in the mid 18th century; the church towers, which are visible from afar, took on their current design in the course of these alterations. In 1744, Johann Anton Quittainer created a Madonna for the façade of this monastery church which is considered to be a masterpiece of Baroque sculpture in Prague.

During the Thirty Years' War, the mortal remains of the founder of the Premonstatensian order and former Bishop of Magdeburg, Norbert of Prémontre, were brought to Prague and buried in this church. In the southern chapel, to the right of the main entrance, rests the Imperial Commander Count of Pappenheim, who was killed in action in 1632 near Lützen and attained immortality through a familiar line in Schiller's Wallenstein: "Therein I rec-

In the courtyard of Strahov Monastery.

A connecting passage, in which a copy of the 9th century Strahov Gospel is exhibited, leads to the Theological Library, the older wing of which was built from 1671–79 by the Italian master builder Giovanni Domenico Orsi de Orsini. The hall derives its name from the mainly theological content of the 16,000 books here.

The panels between the stucco on the ceiling were painted by a member of the order, Frater Siardus Nosecký, between 1723 and 1727. Geographical and astronomical globes have been arranged in the centre of the hall.

The inner monastery is accessed through a gate with a coat of arms, east of the monastery church. A further statue of St Norbert looks down from a niche over the gable. Across the abbey courtyard you reach the former chapter hall and, further on, the Strahov Picture Gallery, where works of such influential Baroque masters as Peter Brandl, Wenzel Lorenz Reiner, Václav Kupetzky and Karel Škréta are exhibited.

The library's Philosophical Hall.

The "Scene of Fire" 2

[Pohořelec] Ⓣ 22 POHOŘELEC

The Pohořelec or "Scene of Fire", which includes Strahov and a part of Petřín Hill, was incorporated into the Castle District under Charles IV. As the district was of considerable strategic importance, it was frequently attacked and damaged by fire more than once, in the course of battles between the Hussites and King Sigismund's Imperial Army in 1420, for example, or during the great fire in the Castle suburb in 1541, and in the battles between Austrian and French troops in 1742. Today however, it is a rather sleepy quarter with a picturesque square surrounded by beautiful buildings from the later Renaissance period and several interesting Baroque and Rococo façades.

The **Nepomuk statue** on the square was created in 1752 by Johann Anton Quittainer. It stood at the Castle Square until 1846.

The **Kutschera Palace** [Pohořelec 22] is a Rococo building from the second half of the 18th century. The former owner, Field Marshall Lieutenant Baron of Kutschera, was acquainted with Ludwig van Beethoven and Emperor Francis I; he even said to have occasionally accompanied the latter on the flute.

The Czech painter Mikoláš Aleš lived in the **"Broad Courtyard"** [Pohořelec 26].

With its superimposed baroque double gables, the Renaissance building **"At the Golden Tree"** [Pohořelec 8] is very striking. A passageway leads through the house into the courtyard of Strahov Monastery.

A palace on the "Scene of Fire".

Czernin Palace

3

[Černínský palác, Loretánské náměstí 5] Ⓣ 22 Pohořelec

Count Humprecht Johann von Černín obtained an ideal plot for a prestigious family palace in 1666. He planned three and a half storeys, spread over a breadth of thirty columns. Three entranceways emphasise the symmetry of this imposing palace, which dominates the dainty Loretto Square like a potentate's fortress. The architect Francesco Caratti was in charge of the construction works until his death in 1677 and the Prague master builder Giovanni de Capauli often employed more than a hundred masons and craftsmen simultaneously at this enormous building site.

Although his successors continued construction after the demise of Humprecht Johann von Černín in 1697, the palace remained unfinished and could never be used as the Černín family seat.

Following severe damage caused during the Bavarian-French occupation (1742) and the Prussian sieges (1744, 1757), the owners tried to sell the colossus to Emperor Joseph II – without success.

Eventually the palace, which had already served as an army hospital during the Napoleonic Wars, was acquired by the military, who converted it into barracks in 1851.

After 1918, the palace was elaborately restored and once again put to a prestigious use: the Ministry of Foreign Affairs moved to Černín Palace. From 1939 to 1944, it was the seat of the Reichsprotektor.

The current Ministry of Foreign Affairs: Černín Palace.

In March 1948, the year of the coup, the then Minister for Foreign Affairs, Jan Masaryk, was found dead beneath one of the palace windows. The circumstances of his death remain mysterious to this day and people refer to it as the Third Defenestration of Prague.

The Ministry of Foreign Affairs still resides in the Černín Palace. Only its garden, with statues by Giovanni Santini-Aichel, is open to the public, and that only on special occasions like concerts and theatre performances in summer.

Loretto Shrine **4**

[Loreta, Loretánské náměstí 7]
Ⓣ 22 POHOŘELEC

According to legend, the house in which the forthcoming birth of the Saviour was announced to the Virgin Mary was threatened by heathens, so it was carried by angels from Nazareth to the small town of Loretto, near Ancona. This pious subject was frequently taken up by the arts, particularly in the Baroque era, giving rise to the foundation of places of pilgrimage across Europe. Fifty such shrines were erected in Bohemia alone.

The best known of these Loretto Shrines, the Prague Loretto, was founded by the Countess Benigna Katherina of Lobkowicz, who came from a wealthy Bohemian family. The attractive west façade built by Kilian Ignaz Dientzenhofer, adorned with elaborate relief ornaments and the (older)

octagonal belfry, dates from the years 1721–22.

In 1694, Eberhard of Glachau, a Prague merchant, spent 15,000 Guilders on having the **carillon** with its 27 bells cast in Amsterdam. The Prague clockmaker Peter Naumann set it in motion in the presence of noted clergy and nobility. It chimes the hymn *We Greet Thee a Thousand Times* on the hour.

In 1661, cloisters were built around the centre of the shrine – the Lauretanian House or **Casa Santa** – in which pilgrims moved from altar to altar reciting the Lauretanian litany.

In the **Chapel of Our Lady of Sorrows** is a rather peculiar cult image: a bearded woman nailed to the cross. It depicts St Wilgefortis, who is said to have refused the heathen who was intended to become her husband. As she

Loretto Shrine in winter.

The bearded virgin.

could find no other way of preserving her virginity, she prayed for visible signs of masculinity – and her prayer was answered. The enraged father had his recalcitrant daughter nailed to the cross.

Detail on the façade of Loretto Church.

The **Church of the Nativity** built by the Dientzenhofers, father and son, a precious gem of Prague Baroque, was given its present shape around 1735. The ceiling, painted with frescoes by Wenzel Lorenz Reiner (Presentation of Jesus in the Temple) and Johann Anton Schöpf (Adoration of the Three Holy Kings; Adoration of the Shepherds) arches over the richly decorated interior of the church.

The valuable Loretto treasure in the **treasure chamber** is mostly a collection of gifts from wealthy noble families. Although the assets have been decimated by wartime losses, the approximately 300 pieces of jewellery, gems, liturgical utensils and ornate monstrances are still enough to delight the most demanding of art lovers.

The oldest object on display is a late Gothic chalice from 1510; the most valuable piece of the collection is the so-called **Diamond Monstrance** ("Prague Sun"). The latter was made in 1699 by the imperial Viennese jewellers to a design by Johann Bernhard Fischer von Erlach. The gilded silver monstrance weighs 12 kg and is set with 6,222 diamonds. A crouching dragon is depicted at the foot of the monstrance symbolising the powers of darkness and evil. The Queen of Heaven, Maria Immaculata, stands on a crescent moon, crowned by 12 stars. She looks at the radiant sun that symbolises God as the light of the world.

Capuchin monastery in Prague.

Capuchin Monastery with the Church of St Mary

5

[Klášter kapucínů, Loretánské náměstí 6] Ⓣ 22 POHOŘELEC

Founded in 1601, this was the first Capuchin monastery in Bohemia. A beautiful statue of St Mary can be found in the affiliated **Church of Our Dear Lady to the Angels**, which in its plainness conforms to the order's ideal of poverty. Every year at Christmas a Baroque crib with semi-life-sized figures is set up in one of the siderooms.

New World

6

[Nový Svět] Ⓣ 22 BRUSNICE

In the 16th century, a humble settlement emerged on the northern outskirts of the Castle District, over the ditch of the Brusnice stream: the "New World". The area has retained its romantic appeal although the small houses in the narrow lane have burned down several times over the course of the centuries. The people living here were certainly not wealthy, but they were happy to have a roof over their heads. No wonder they were proud enough to consider their dwellings "golden"! Since then, however, the picturesque New World

Past and present in the New World.

House "At the Golden Grape".

has become an upmarket artist's quarter, whose tranquillity is a pleasant contrast to the lively bustle of the Golden Lane.

The Baroque house "**At the Golden Plough**" [Nový Svět 25] was built in the 17th century. The Czech violin virtuoso František Ondříček was born here in 1857.

The house "**At the White Lion**" [Nový Svět 21] has a very beautiful courtyard overgrown with ivy.

The house "**At the Golden Grape**" [Nový Svět 5] dates from the 17th century and is guarded by a fierce looking predatory fish on the oriole.

The house "**At the Golden Pear**" [Nový Svět 3] is a Baroque building from the 18th century and houses a traditional tavern, hence the decoration on the façade: ears of corn and grapevines stand for food and drink.

The imperial astronomer Tycho de Brahe is said to have lived "**At the Golden Griffin**" [Nový Svět 1] around 1600.

Church of St John of Nepomuk at Prague Castle **7**

[Kostel sv. Jana z Nepomuku, Kanovnická] Ⓣ 22 BRUSNICE

This church, built between 1720 and 1728 on a cruciform ground plan, was the first place of worship in Prague to be designed by the Baroque architect Kilian Ignaz Dientzenhofer. The ceiling frescoes were executed by Wenzel Lorenz Reiner and show scenes from the life of St Nepomuk. The church and the affiliated Ursuline convent were closed down in the course of the Josephine Reforms and put to use for military purposes. After 1902, the building became a Catholic garrison church as well as a barracks.

The most prominent officer to serve in the barracks was Colonel and Crown Prince Rudolph von Habsburg, who came here as Commanding Officer of Infantry Regiment no. 36 from 1879 on.

Canons' Lane **8**

[Kanovnická] Ⓣ 22 BRUSNICE

The **Austrian Residency** [Kanovnická 4] is a medieval building which

The Austrian Residency.

was remodelled in the Renaissance style around 1600 and again in the Baroque manner in 1690 by Albrecht Hložek of Žampach, Captain of the Castle. Today the palace, with its beautiful gardens, is the official residence of the ambassador of the Austrian Republic. The magnificence of old Austria, however, can, on special occasions, still be felt in the sumptuous reception rooms.

The sgraffitoed **House of Pages** [Kanovnická 3] was used to accommodate the Imperial pages.

Castle Square   9

[Hradčanské náměstí]
Ⓣ 22 PRAŽSKÝ HRAD

The **Marian column** at the centre of the Castle Square was created in 1726 and erected here in 1736 as a plague column, and probably also as a tangible symbol of the victorious counter-reformation. The saints underneath the towering Immaculata – John of Nepomuk, Elizabeth, Peter, Norbert, Florian, Charles Borro-

meus, Wenceslas, Vitus and Adalbert – came from Ferdinand Maximilian Brokoff's workshop.

The **Tuscany Palace** [Hradčanské náměstí 5] was owned by the Dukes of Tuscany after 1718. At the corner facing Loretto Lane is a group of Baroque sculptures depicting Archangel Michael with the flaming sword. Each of the two entrances to this two-winged building boasts a ducal coat of arms crowned with a cornucopia.

Martinic Palace [Hradčanské náměstí 8] was built by the same Jaroslav Bořita of Martinic who was thrown out of the window of the Bohemian Chancellery. Renaissance sgraffitos on its façade show scenes from the Bible and classical mythology.

The **Canon's Residence** [Hradčanské náměstí 10] was once occupied by the Swabian cathedral master builder Peter Parler, whom Emperor Charles IV entrusted with the construction of St Vitus' Cathedral after the death of the first master builder, Matthew of Arras.

Sternberg Palace [Hradčanské náměstí 15] can be accessed through an entrance adjacent to the Archbishop's Palace. Wenzel Adalbert, Count Sternberg had this simple

The Castle Square, seen from St Vitus Cathedral.

The Archbishop's Palace; in the background the spires of St Vitus' Cathedral.

four-winged complex built in the years 1695–1720.

The **Archbishop's Palace** [Hradčanské náměstí 16] is a late Baroque palace based on a Renaissance structure. Sculptures by Ignaz Franz Platzer, five balconies and a coat of arms adorn the impressive façade. The Archbishops of Prague have resided here since 1562.

The **Salm Palace** [Hradčanské náměstí 1] is an Empire-style palace connected to the neighbouring Schwarzenberg Palace.

Schwarzenberg Palace.

The **Schwarzenberg Palace** [Hradčanské náměstí 2] was built in the Florentine style by Johann Count Lobkowicz between 1545 and 1563. For many years, the sgraffitoed palace accomodated an army museum, now it is home to the National Gallery.

The **Carmelite Convent** [Hradčanské náměstí 3] has belonged to the Barefooted Carmelites since 1792.

Royal Gardens   **10**
[Královské zahrady, Pražský hrad]
Ⓣ 22 PRAŽSKÝ HRAD

The Royal Gardens are reached through a wrought-iron gate opposite the Riding School (next to the Lion Courtyard, formerly an enclosure for predatory animals). The gardens were laid out by Emperor Ferdinand I and his successors in the 16th century, as a replacement for old vineyards, and now exude the charm of an English park. When they were first laid out, however, and the first tulips in Central Europe blossomed here, the Royal Gardens must have been a Renaissance paradise; this idyll prospered into the Baroque 18th century until it was destroyed in times of war.

The first building to the right, surrounded by chestnut trees, is the **Presidential Residence**. In the late 1940s, an additional wing was built onto Kilian Ignaz Dientzenhofer's greenhouse. A short distance ahead is the sgraffitoed **Royal Ballroom Hall** [Míčovna], built between 1567 and 1569 by Bonifaz Wolmut, and formerly an open loggia structure. Next to it is the **Oran-**

The Royal Ballroom Hall.

gery, vaulted by a modernistic glass and steel construction.

Royal Summer Residence "Belvedere" 11

[Letohrádek královny Anny, Pražský hrad] Ⓣ 22 KRÁLOVSKÝ LETOHRÁDEK

This marvellous summer residence was a gift of Emperor Ferdinand I to his wife Anna Jagiello. It was begun in 1534 and completed over a period of more

than two decades in the Lombardic Renaissance style.

The surrounding arcades are decorated with a multitude of reliefs and heraldic motifs depicting scenes from classical mythology and national history. The interior of this summer palace contains two domed Renaissance halls on the ground floor and a ballroom hall with a wooden coffered ceiling upstairs. One of the peculiarities of the hall is the cycle of mural paintings with motifs drawn from Bohemian national history.

In front of the Belvedere Summer Residence, which is nowadays used as a venue for exhibitions, the **Singing Fountain** cast in 1568 attracts the attention of passers-by. The name refers to the sound of the water falling into the bronze basin rather than to the piper who stands on top of the fountain. Scenes from antique mythology are depicted on the base of the fountain.

"Belvedere" Summer Residence in the Royal Gardens.

Prague Castle
[Pražský hrad]

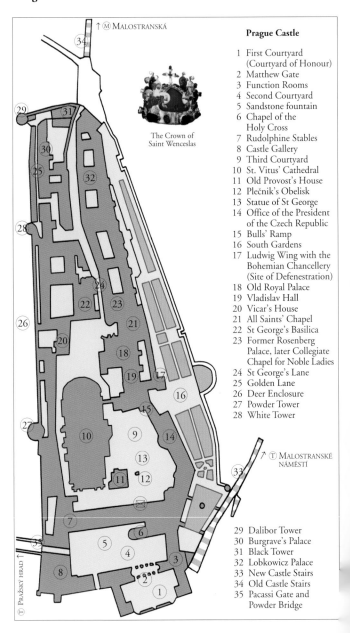

The Crown of
Saint Wenceslas

Prague Castle

1 First Courtyard
   (Courtyard of Honour)
2 Matthew Gate
3 Function Rooms
4 Second Courtyard
5 Sandstone fountain
6 Chapel of the
   Holy Cross
7 Rudolphine Stables
8 Castle Gallery
9 Third Courtyard
10 St. Vitus' Cathedral
11 Old Provost's House
12 Plečnik's Obelisk
13 Statue of St George
14 Office of the President
   of the Czech Republic
15 Bulls' Ramp
16 South Gardens
17 Ludwig Wing with the
   Bohemian Chancellery
   (Site of Defenestration)
18 Old Royal Palace
19 Vladislav Hall
20 Vicar's House
21 All Saints' Chapel
22 St George's Basilica
23 Former Rosenberg
   Palace, later Collegiate
   Chapel for Noble Ladies
24 St George's Lane
25 Golden Lane
26 Deer Enclosure
27 Powder Tower
28 White Tower

29 Dalibor Tower
30 Burgrave's Palace
31 Black Tower
32 Lobkowicz Palace
33 New Castle Stairs
34 Old Castle Stairs
35 Pacassi Gate and
   Powder Bridge

Prague Castle
[Pražský Hrad]

First Castle Courtyard 🔲 12
Ⓣ 22 Pražský hrad

The "**Courtyard of Honour**" is entered through a wrought-iron gate which bears the monograms of the Empress Maria Theresia and her son Joseph II and is guarded by two regimental sentries. The two battling Titans that flank the gate were carved by the Rococo sculptor Ignaz Franz Platzer in 1770; the original figures were replaced with replicas in 1921.

The wings of the building originate from the second half of the 18th century and their austerity marks the end of Prague Baroque. At that time, after the Seven Years' War against Prussia, Empress Maria Theresia placed the reconstruction of the Imperial Palace into the capable hands of Viennese architect Nicolo Pacassi.

Giant at the Castle gate.

The **Matthew Gate** (1614) in contrast, is considered to be the earliest example of Prague Baroque. Emperor Matthew I entrusted the famous Italian master builder Vincenzo Scamozzi with its construction. Pacassi had the previous castle gate incorporated into the new entrance section.

Castle

The Matthew Gate at the entrance to the second Castle Courtyard.

The slim flagpoles are a foretaste of the Slovene architect Josip Plečnik's concept of form.
From the passage to the second Castle Courtyard, a stately staircase on the right leads up to the **function rooms**, formerly the Imperial Chambers. To the left, a newer staircase leads to one of the porticos designed by Josip Plečnik. From here there is access to other stately rooms, such as the Rothmayer Hall, the Spanish Hall and the Rudolph Gallery.

Most of the function rooms, however, are not open to the public. Only a select few are permitted to view the Throne Hall, the Habsburg, Brožík, Mirror, Music, Social, or Čermák Salons.

Second Castle Courtyard **13**

Ⓣ 22 PRAŽSKÝ HRAD

The early Baroque **sandstone fountain** in the Second Courtyard was created by the Prague-based stonemason Hieronymus Kohl and the Italian Francesco della Torre. This fountain, at the feet of four Roman gods (Vulcan, Hercules, Neptune, and Mercury), was crowned with an Imperial eagle until 1918.

Sandstone fountain
in the Castle Courtyard.

In recent years (1961–1990), the treasure of St Vitus' Cathedral was stored in the **Chapel of the Holy Cross**. The late Baroque chapel was built by Anselmo Lurago, who relied largely on the plans of court architect Pacassi.

In the 19th century, the chapel was reconstructed in a Classicist manner. The religious artwork in the interior and expecially the painting of the crucifixion at the altar are particularly noteworthy.

The Chapel of the Holy Cross was the family chapel of the unfortunate monarch Ferdinand I, who lived in quiet seclusion at Prague Castle following his abdication in 1848.

Facing the Chapel is the entrance to the **Castle Gallery**, where significant pieces of the Imperial collections are exhibited (among them paintings by Rubens, Tintoretto, Titian and Veronese). The Rudolphine Stables to the north are also used as exhibition venues.

Third Castle Courtyard

St Vitus' Cathedral **14**

[Chrám sv. Víta, Pražský hrad]
Ⓣ 22 PRAŽSKÝ HRAD

In the 11th century, a three-nave basilica replaced an earlier Romanesque rotunda. It was to serve as the church where the Přemyslid dynasty were crowned and buried.

In 1344, Emperor Charles IV entrusted the French architect Matthew of Arras with the construction of a new Gothic cathedral. After his unexpected death in 1352, the Swabian Peter Parler continued the building work with a substantially altered design. The Hussite wars brought construction work to a standstill in 1419. It was only to be completed in the 20th century by the

Castle

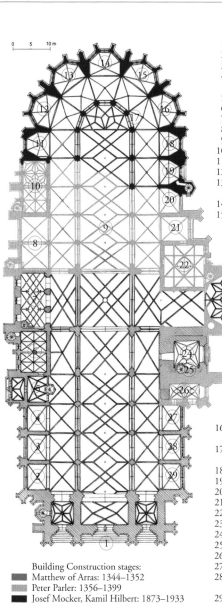

St Vitus' Cathedral

1 Entrance
2 St Agnes Chapel
3 Schwarzenberg Chapel
4 Archbishops' Chapel with Mucha-Window
5 Treasury
6 New Registry
7 Choir Chapel
8 St Sigismund Chapel
9 Royal Mausoleum
10 Old Registry
11 St Anna Chapel
12 Pernstein Chapel
13 Chapel of St John the Baptist
14 Emperor's Chapel
15 Saxon Chapel

16 Tomb of St John of Nepomuk
17 St John of Nepomuk Chapel
18 Wallenstein Chapel
19 Royal Oratory
20 Holy Cross Chapel
21 St Andrew Chapel
22 St Wenceslas Chapel
23 Golden Gate
24 Hasenburg Chapel
25 Access to belfry
26 Chapter Library
27 Thun Chapel
28 Chapel of the Holy Grave
29 St Ludmila Chapel

Building Construction stages:
▓ Matthew of Arras: 1344–1352
▓ Peter Parler: 1356–1399
■ Josef Mocker, Kamil Hilbert: 1873–1933

master cathedral builders Kamil Hilbert and Josef Mocker in a neo-Gothic style. The official opening ceremony of the 124 m long cathedral took place in 1929. The west front of the cathedral is adorned with statues and overlooked by two 82 m high neo-Gothic spires. The church can be entered through three exquisitely detailed portals with relief decorated bronze doors.

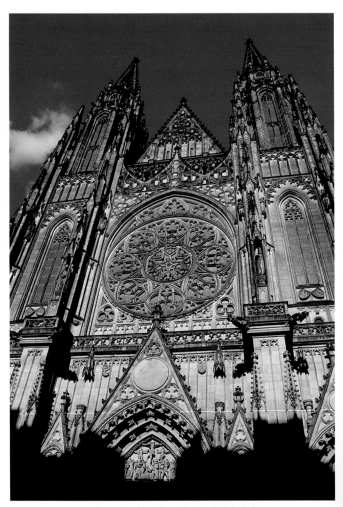

The neo-Gothic spires of St Vitus' Cathedral.

Bust of Charles IV on the triforium.

The national arms painted on the arcade walls of the choir convey an impression of the extent of the Habsburg hereditary dominions in the 17th century.

Several dozen animal heads, mascarones and portraits of eminent personalities look down at the beholder from the inner and outer **triforium** and the chancel, among them portraits of Emperor Charles IV and his wives, as well as busts of the cathedral's master builders Peter Parler and Matthew of Arras.

It would go beyond the scope of this book to describe in detail all the art treasures and the peculiarities of the various chapels of St Vitus' Cathedral (The **St Sigismund Chapel** with the relics of St Sigismund; the **St Anna Chapel** facing Georg Bendl's wooden relief carving portraying the flight of "Winter King" Frederick of the Palatinate after the Battle at White Mountain; the **Pernstein Chapel**, which is the burial chapel of the Archbishops of Prague; the **Saxon Chapel** with the tombs of the Přemysl kings Otakar I and II; the **St Nepomuk Chapel** opposite the silver statue of St Nepomuk created by Fischer von Erlach; the **Wallenstein Chapel** with the crypt of the Wallensteins, a famous Bohemian noble family; the **Chapel of the Holy Cross**, which gives access to the royal crypt and much more). By far the most important of the cathedral's chapels, however, is the high Gothic **St Wenceslas Chapel**. The burial chapel of St Wenceslas is

Inside, the visitor faces the overwhelming panorama of a Gothic cathedral: the neo-Gothic construction of the nave merges almost seamlessly into the medieval section of the choir, which is bathed in warm light.

The **Royal Mausoleum**, made of white marble in 1589, is situated in the chancel of St Vitus' Cathedral, in front of the neo-Gothic high altar and the ornamental Baroque choir stalls. It is enclosed by particularly artistic Renaissance lattice-work. The individual parts of the mausoleum were created in Innsbruck and brought to Prague by sledge and boat. The royal majesties resting in the tomb have been depicted lovingly and in rich detail on its outside: the Habsburgian Ferdinand I flanked by his wife, Anna Jagiello, and his son, Maximilian II. The relief medallions on the side show the rulers who were formerly buried under the mausoleum: Charles IV (and his wives), Wenceslas IV, Ladislav Postumus and George of Poděbrady.

Statue of St Wenceslas
in the St Wenceslas Chapel.

north, with decorative mouldings by Peter Parler. Another noteworthy door is inside the chapel: the entrance to the **Crown Chamber**. Behind its seven locks are kept the coronation insignia of the Bohemian kings (crown, Imperial orb and sceptre). Only very rarely, and on special occasions, is the chamber opened to the public. This happened only eight times in the 20th century.

From the **Hasenburg Chapel**, situated to the south, there is access to the spiral staircase leading to the upper levels of the belfry and the bells. The panorama from the top is unique! It is well worth braving the narrow stairwell with 285 steps solely for this incredible view.

splendidly decorated and contains several valuable works of art, such as the medieval statue of the saint.

Wenceslas I, whose dead body was brought to the St Vitus' Rotunda on the orders of his brother (and murderer) Boleslav I, had expressed the wish during his lifetime to be buried in this church after his death. Peter Parler erected the sumptuous chapel over the saint's grave on the orders of Emperor Charles IV. Between the cornice and the base, the chapel walls are adorned with valuable murals and gilded stucco decorations as well as more than 1,300 emeralds and semiprecious stones of all colours.

There are two entrances to the chapel. The 20th century wrought-iron portal to the west contrasts with the Gothic portal to the

The southern exterior of the cathedral is dominated by the large copper-topped St Vitus' **belfry**. The characteristic shape of the roof was

The cathedral's belfry.

St Vitus' Cathedral at night
(choir with chapels).

created by the Renaissance master builder Bonifaz Wolmut. The heaviest bell in the country, weighing 18 tons, has hung behind a lancet window with a gilded ornamental grille since 1549; it is known as "Sigismund".

The crowned "R" above the window of the belfry is a reminder of the legendary Habsburg Emperor Rudolph II, whose fate was so closely linked to that of Prague Castle. Three stone coats of arms have been placed beneath the window: to the left, the double-tailed Bohemian lion, in the centre, the flaming eagle of St Wenceslas (the former Bohemian heraldic beast) and to the right, the archbishop of Prague's coat of arms. The time can be read from two dials, each with just one hand: the upper one indicating the hour, the lower one the minutes and quarters of the hour.

Adjacent to the belfry is the world famous **Golden Gate** (Porta aurea), which leads inside the cathedral. A glass mosaic, created by Venetian craftsmen on behalf of Emperor Charles IV, sparkles over three pointed arches in 30 different colours. The mosaic is a reminder of the Last Judgement and the blazing flames of purgatory. A delegation of Bohemian patron saints looks up at the saviour. Emperor Charles IV and his wife Elizabeth of Pomerania can be seen in the spandrel below, they too are present at the judgement.

From the Cathedral Square, the bull stairs of Josip Plečnik grant entry to the **South Gardens** (Rampart and Paradise Gardens). The garden complex offers an abundance of marvellous details and great vistas of the historical city centre. Plečnik conjured up a unique garden world with fountains, pavilions, steps, lawns, pyramids, obelisks – you can spend hours studying the characteristic shapes of the Slovene castle architect and enjoying the interplay of art and nature.

Old Provost's House 15

[Staré proboštství, Pražský hrad]
(T) 22 PRAŽSKÝ HRAD

On the southwest corner of St Vitus Cathedral is the Old Provost's House of the cathedral chapter, the former seat of the

The Old Provost's House.

bishops in Prague. The building originates from the 18th century, though the **statue of St Wenceslas** on its corner is older (1662); it is the work of Johann G. Bendl, the leading Prague Baroque sculptor and carver of his day.

Plečnik's Obelisk 16

[Plečnikův obelisk, Pražský hrad]
Ⓣ 22 PRAŽSKÝ HRAD

In 1928, on the tenth anniversary of the republic, an almost 17 m high obelisk was erected opposite the Old Provost's House to commemorate the victims of the Great War. Architect Josip Plečnik chose an enormous block of Mrákotín granite for the obelisk. However, his original plan to place an allegorical sculpture on top and to lay a grave for the Un-

known Soldier at the foot of the column was not carried out. To this day the monument has remained unfinished.

St George's Statue 17

[Socha sv. Jiří, Pražský hrad]
Ⓣ 22 PRAŽSKÝ HRAD

The statue of St George on horseback by the brothers Martin and Georg of Klausenburg in 1373 is the most important sculpture in the third Castle Courtyard. It is, however, only a replica. It stands on a diorite plinth by Josip Plečnik.

The original statue is on display in the nearby St George's Convent. The saint is shown in the act of slaying a dragon with his lance; his horse was destroyed in a tournament in 1562, so we cannot be certain how faithful the replica actually is to the original.

Opposite the statue of St George is a covered archaeological site. In the course of extensive excavations in the 1920s, valuable old stonework was discovered, since when it has been left open to public view. The walls date back to the 11th century and form parts of the foundations of the former Bishop's Chapel of St Mauritius and St Vitus' Basilica. Josip Plečnik created the reinforced concrete construction that secures the site.

Statue of St George.

Old Royal Palace

[Starý královský palác Jiřské náměstí 33] Ⓣ 22 PRAŽSKÝ HRAD

The origins of this palace go back to the 1ˢᵗ century AD. The intricate architectonic ensemble of the building provides an impressive reflection of the stylistic periods of past centuries.

From the entrance hall, one steps into the ground level function floor. After a glance into the "**Green Chamber**" to the left, where the royal court was held, and into the small audience hall (the so-called "Vladislavian Bedchamber"), a special treat awaits the visitor: the **Vladislav Hall** created by the Austrian Benedikt von Ried around 1500, on the cusp of the Renaissance. The Throne Hall has been the scene of many a ceremonial meeting

The so-called Bohemian Chancellery.

and is the place where the great of the nation attended tournaments of knights mounted on noble steeds. To this day, the splendidly vaulted hall serves as a representative venue for ceremonious occasions, whether Presidential elections or grand receptions for important state guests.

Vladislav Hall in the Old Royal Palace.

From the southwest corner of the Vladislav Hall, there is access to the so-called Ludwig Wing with the two rooms of the **Bohemian Chancellery**. Behind a crowned portal bearing the initial "L" for Louis Jagiello, waits a room with a charged history: on May 23rd 1618, two Imperial governors were plunged into the depths from a window in the east wall of the former Chancellery (Second Defenestration of Prague).

Since around 1600, a passageway adorned with coats of arms has connected the Vladislav Hall to the **All Saints Chapel**, whose origins date from the 12th century. After the great fire in 1541 the chapel was rebuilt in its present shape and was subsequently (in 1755) designated as the collegiate chapel for noble ladies residing in the neighbourhood.

The Baroque high altar is fitted with an altarpiece by Wenzel Lorenz Reiner. A cycle of paintings executed by Christian Dittmann tells the legend of St Procopius, whose relics were brought to Prague Castle in 1588 from the Benedictine monastery of Sázava, where he had been abbot. The saint's Baroque monument, surrounded by allegories of virtue, stands in a recess in the north wall of the chapel. The painting *Deposition from the Cross* on the side-altar to the right is attributed to the Rudolphine court artist Hans von Aachen.

Climbing the spiral staircase from the entrances at the north end of the Vladislav Hall, you reach the chambers of the "**New Royal Register**", which are decorated with coats of arms, and the **Old Chamber of Common Law**. It

View of Prague Castle; in the foreground (left of the centre) is the Old Royal Palace.

was rebuilt by Bonifaz Wolmut with very decorative Gothic tracery after the fire of 1541. When parliament assembled here, the representatives of the Estates sat on the upholstered benches, while the throne with the Bohemian lions was reserved for the king.

We leave the Vladislav Hall and the Royal Palace via the Riders' Staircase, with its arched rib-vaulting by Benedikt von Ried; the route the mounted tournament participants would also have taken in days of yore.

St George's Basilica   **19**
[Kostel sv. Jiří, Pražský hrad]
Ⓣ 22 Pražský hrad

The foundations of the basilica originate from the 12th century the brick-red façade behind which the Romanesque choir towers rise is, however, early Baroque. St George the Dragon Slayer stands guard in the tympanum at the front, while a statue of St Nepomuk looks down at the visitors from the portal ledge of the chapel, which was built in the early 18th century.

The basilica is connected to George's Lane [Jiřská] by an early Renaissance gateway, dating from the beginning of the 16th century; again, its tympanum depicts St George battling the dragon.

In the Romanesque interior of the church with its ceiling of wooden beams, there are Přemyslid tombs. The founder of the church Vratislav I (died 921) is buried here in a striking tomb.

The beautifully painted **Choir Chapel of St Ludmila** houses the tomb of St Wenceslas' grandmother. The stone figure on the tomb reminds us of St Ludmila's martyrdom; in 925, she was attacked in her sanctuary at Tetín, not far from Prague, and was strangled with her veil.

A cross-vaulted Romanesque **crypt** awaits us beneath the choir loft. An allegory to vanity dating from the 16th century is preserved here: snakes and revolting swarms of vermin crawl around the decomposing entrails of a human body.

The dome of the **Nepomuk Chapel** was painted with the apotheosis of the saint by Wenzel Lorenz Reiner in 1722; both altar pieces are also his work. On

Castle

St George's Basilica, as seen from the belfry of St Vitus' Cathedral.

Defence towers of the Castle: Daliborka (round tower) and Black Tower.

the chapel walls there are scenes from the life of St Nepomuk; the saint's statue on the portal was created by Ferdinand Maximilian Brokoff.

The National Gallery displays a collection of Bohemian Mannerism and Baroque art in the early Baroque convent neighbouring the basilica.

Golden Lane ▪20▪

[Zlatá ulička, Pražský hrad]
Ⓣ 22 Pražský hrad

The medieval fortified wall over the ditch of the Brusnice stream behind the Castle provided Vladislav Jagiello with the basis for a small picturesque lane, the Goldmakers' Lane. Goldsmiths probably lived in the dwellings which were built beneath the fortified wall in the 15th century, thus the name "Goldsmith Lane" gained currency. Rudolf II had the miserable huts and houses demolished and permitted 24 members of the castle guard to make their dwellings in the blind arcades beneath the battlemented parapet.

The so-called "**White Tower**", an artillery tower at the west end of the Goldmakers' Lane, can be reached via the battlemented parapet whose crenelles enabled the northern defence of the Castle in the 15th century. During the rule of Emperor Rudolph II this tower was a dark dungeon; on the ground floor above the dungeons was a torture chamber. The English alchemist and charlatan Edward Kelley was one of the legendary inmates.

Probably the best known resident of the Golden Lane was Franz Kafka, who was based at no. 22

Castle

The Golden Lane at Prague Castle.

Kafka's cottage in Golden Lane (no. 22).

for several months in 1916–17; among the pieces he worte here are the narrations collected in *A Country Doctor*. Kafka used to spend the evening hours in the cottage although he couldn't stay overnight in the small, sparsely furnished room. A small bookshop has been set up here in honour of the writer.

The **Dalibor Tower** [Daliborka] is another artillery tower forming part of the northerly defence complex. There were also prisons and deep dark dungeons in this tower which rises high above the deer enclosure. The Knight Dalibor of Kozojedy was among those imprisoned here. The unfortunate knight attained fame beyond the country's borders through Bedřich Smetana's romantic opera *Dalibor*.

Burgrave's Palace 21

[Purkrabství, Jiřská 4]
Ⓣ 22 PRAŽSKÝ HRAD

The former Burgrave's Palace is situated in George's Lane [Jiřská]. Coats of arms carved in stone over the entrance portal are a reminder of the families that once held this honourable office. The main building of the Burgraviate stands besides more recent buildings in the extensive grounds along with the "**Black Tower**", known in the Middle Ages as the "Golden Tower" because of its gilt lead roof.

Opposite the Burgrave's Palace is the **castle-palace of the Lobkowicz family**, an early Baroque palace whose magnificent halls are venues for concerts and exhibitions.

Façade detail at no. 22 Golden Lane: "Franz Kafka lived here".

The Old Castle Stairway connects the eastern part of the Castle to the Lesser Town.

The Lesser Town
[Malá Strana]

A Walk through the Lesser Town

[Malá Strana]

The narrow lanes, squares and gardens of this picturesque part of the city lie at the foot of two dominant hills: the Castle Hill, with Prague Castle, borders the Lesser Town to the north, the wooded Petřín Hill forms the boundary to the south.

The first traces of settlement in the Lesser Town are found in the area of Bridge Lane [Mostecká] and the Lesser Town Square [Malostranské náměstí] and date back to the first millenium. The Lesser Town was eventually established in 1257 by Přemysl Otakar II, who had it fortified and enclosed by a wall. Under the rule of Charles IV, this part of the city was extended considerably southwards to Petřín Hill and enclosed by the Hunger Wall built about 1360.

Because the Lesser Town acted as a strategic perimeter for the defence of the Castle, it was devastated during the Hussite wars. The warring sides deliberately destroyed the buildings so that the enemy could not find cover. After the Hussites took over Prague Castle on 7th July 1421, this part of the city was nothing but an expanse of rubble. The decimated citizenry were only able to rebuild and repair the ruins of the Lesser Town of Prague many years later.

When King Vladislav Jagiello moved the royal seat back to the Castle from the Old Town in 1484, the strategic position of the Lesser Town put it in danger once more. Armed conflicts were not the only thing to be feared, however:

On the afternoon of the 2nd June 1541 a fire broke out in the Lesser Town Square, rapidly spread across the surrounding areas and soon developed into the most devastating conflagration in the history of Prague. The disastrous fire of 1541, which burned two thirds of the buildings in the Lesser Town and also large parts of Prague Castle to the ground, entirely changed the appearance of the Lesser Town. The ruins were rebuilt in the Renaissance style then in vogue, and even buildings spared by the fire were remodelled after contemporary tastes.

Under the Habsburg crown, and especially after the Battle of White Mountain, the Lesser Town took on an increasingly feudal character. Many unfortunate Protestant noble families had to leave the town; Catholic aristocrats came to replace them and primarily settled in the immediate vicinity of the Imperial Castle. They built mansions and palaces in the Lesser Town, living out their expectations of a suitable lifestyle in the quiet lanes.

After the misery of the Thirty Years' War, a new era had dawned, whose new lease of life was reflected in the opulent forms of the Baroque.

A look at the Lesser Town in winter (St Nicholas' towers to the right; St Thomas' on the left).

Within one single generation dozens of buildings and monuments emerged, and this period moulded the appearance of the Lesser Town like no other to this day.

With the 18th century drawing to a close, the days of the Baroque period were numbered. Catholic dominance began to crumble and the nobility lost its supremacy to a strengthened citizenry who gained in influence and affluence in the course of industrialisation of the 19th century. The Lesser Town, however, following its integration into the union of the four cities of Prague in 1784, became a rather sleepy district, spared the hustle and bustle of the 19th century, and its quiet magic prevails here even today. A maze of tiny lanes, proud palaces, fragrant gardens and quiet churches: the Lesser Town is the gentle heart of a bustling city.

The Lesser Town Square seen from the tower of St Nicholas'.

A view from the Castle forecourt over the roofs of the Lesser Town.

View of the Lesser Town; in the background (centre) is Strahov Monastery.

Lesser Town Square 22
[Malostranské náměstí] Ⓣ 12, 20, 22

In the days of Emperor Rudolph II, the Lesser Town Square was known as the "Italian Square" and between 1859 and 1918 as "Radetzky Square", named after the famous Austrian Field Marshall. The Baroque **St Nicholas' Church** divides the square into two parts: Since 1715, the upper part has been adorned with a

Trinity column to serve as a reminder of the dangers of the plague, now overcome.

The lower part of the square is dominated by the **"Grömling" Palace** with its magnificent Baroque façade. The venerable "Café Radetzky", later known as "Malostranská kavárna", has been situated here since the 19th century.

The **Kaiserstein Palace** [Malostranské náměstí 23] is decorated with

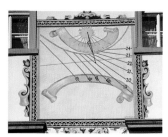

Detail of a Lesser Town façade:
A sundial shows the time.

A maze of roofs and chimneys
in the Lesser Town.

St Nicholas' Church in the Lesser Town.

The (former) Lesser Town Hall.

The busy Neruda Lane.

Lesser Town

allegories of the seasons. A bust commemorates Emma Destinnová, one of Enrico Caruso's partners.

The **Lesser Town Hall** [Malostranské náměstí 21] was the seat of the Lesser Town self-administration until the union of the four Prague cities.

Liechtenstein Palace [Malostranské náměstí 13] is a Renaissance building with a classicist façade and was the Imperial Governor's seat until 1918.

St Nicholas' Church in the Lesser Town [23]

[Kostel sv. Mikuláše, Malostranské nám.]
Ⓣ 12, 20, 22 MALOSTRANSKÉ NÁMĚSTÍ

With its impressive dome and 79 m high belfry, St Nicholas' Church rises in the centre of the Lesser Town Square. This church is the most significant creation of high Baroque in Prague and was built between 1673 and 1755 on behalf of the Jesuits. It is a magnificent masterpiece of the Bavarian master builders Christoph and Kilian Ignaz Dientzenhofer.

The church interior is decorated with lavish splendour. A gilt statue of St Nicholas made by Ignaz Franz Platzer is set on the high altar, the side altars are fitted with pieces created by the most im-

portant Baroque artists; the nave is painted with arresting frescoes. The ceiling fresco is one of the largest of its kind in Europe and spreads over some 1,500 m^2.

Neruda Lane [24]

[Nerudova]
Ⓣ 12, 20, 22 MALOSTRANSKÉ NÁMĚSTÍ

Neruda Lane is a road way from the Lesser Town Square up towards the Castle. The steep lane bears the name of the important Prague writer Jan Neruda, who lived here, finding the models for the characters in his famous

Famous house symbol in Nerudova: "At the Three Violins".

"At the Two Suns": the Czech author Jan Neruda lived here.

The house **"At the Golden Lion"** [Nerudova 32] is home to a museum of pharmacy.

The legendary advocate Franz Josef von Bretfeld held glittering balls in the Palace **"At Summer and Winter"** [Nerudova 33]. Mozart and his wife Constanze were guests here in 1787.

The house **"At the Red Lion"** [Nerudova 45] has no entrance of its own. It has to be accessed through the neighbouring house.

The house **"At the Two Suns"** [Nerudova 47] was the home of Czech poet Jan Neruda.

Tales from the Little Quarter. The street was previously known as "Spur Makers' Lane", after the resident craftsmen. A particularly large number of original Prague house symbols can still be found here. They were commonly used as addresses before the present-day house numbers were introduced.

The **Černín-Morzin Palace** dates from around 1670. The two Moorish figurines (hinting at the meaning of the family name of Morzin) on the portal were made by Ferdinand Maximilian Brokoff. Today the Romanian embassy is based in the palace.

The impressive **Thun-Hohenstein Palace** [Nerudova 20] was created by Giovanni Santini-Aichel (1677–1723); its magnificent Baroque portal shows two enormous eagles spreading their wings. The Italian Embassy has been located here since 1921. Adjacent to the palace is the Church of St Mary, built by the Theatine order in 1672. This order was among those dissolved by Emperor Joseph II.

Wallenstein Palace and Garden   **25**

[Valdštejnský palác, Valdštejnské nám. 4]
Ⓣ 12, 20, 22 MALOSTRANSKÉ NÁMĚSTÍ

One of the largest building projects in the Lesser Town was the palace of Imperial Generalissimo Albrecht von Wallenstein. He ob-

Wallenstein Palace from the front.

The Sala terrena of Wallenstein Palace.

Bronze horse in the Wallenstein Garden.

artificial stalagtites can be found in the spacious grounds. The **bronze replicas** of original statues by Adrian de Fries (from 1622 to 1626) have found an almost ideal venue in the garden. The originals were taken by Swedish troops to their homeland during the Thirty Years' War. In recent years, the Senate of the Czech Republic has assembled in the Wallenstein Palace which has been adapted for this purpose.

Church and Monastery of St Thomas `26`

[Kostel a klášter sv. Tomáše, Letenská]
Ⓣ 12, 20, 22 MALOSTRANSKÉ NÁMĚSTÍ

Lesser Town

tained an extensive tract of land in the neighbourhood of the Augustine monastery in the 1620s and had a many-winged palace built on the site in the late Renaissance style. Altogether, 23 buildings, a brickyard and several gardens had to make way for the complex.

It consists of three courtyards and an extensive garden. 300 saddle- and cart horses were permanently housed in the **Wallenstein stables** and even the feeding troughs were made of marble.

Well worth a visit is the beautiful **audience hall** on the first floor of the palace, which is fitted with a ceiling fresco depicting the Duke of Wallenstein himself, riding triumphantly in a Roman carriage and adorned with a laurel wreath.

The architecturally significant fresco-decorated **Sala terrena** faces the gardens. A large aviary with peculiar

The Gothic church originally built for the Benedictine monks was badly damaged during the Hussite wars. Kilian Ignaz Dientzenhofer had the church remodelled in the Baroque style

St Thomas' Church.

97

between 1723 and 1731, thus creating its present appearance. A statue of St Augustine by Hieronymus Kohl is placed over the main gate. Scenes from the life of St Augustine are depicted in the ceiling frescoes by Wenzel Lorenz Reiner inside the church. The pulpit and main altar are attributed to Johann Anton Quittainer, while the altar pieces are copies of later works by Rubens. After 1285, the monastery belonged to the order of Augustinian hermits. The order was granted brewing rights in 1352 and the monastery was home to Prague's oldest brewery until 1953.

Kaunitz Palace `27`

[Kounický palác, Mostecká 15]
Ⓣ 12, 20, 22 MALOSTRANSKÉ NÁMĚSTÍ

Baroque façades dominate the lively Bridge Lane, but the foundations of the townhouses and palaces often date back to medieval times. Thus by comparison, the proud Kaunitz Palace, built in 1773–1775, is rather young. Today it is home to the embassy of the Republic of Serbia. The palace is adorned with stucco and sculptures from Ignaz Franz Platzer's workshop.

Schönborn Palace `28`

[Schönbornský palác, Tržiště 15]
Ⓣ 12, 20, 22 MALOSTRANSKÉ NÁMĚSTÍ

This palace is home to the American embassy today and was built in the 17th century; it acquired its present-day appearance around 1715.

The garden, which ascends towards Petřín Hill, is particularly magnificent and its gloriette is visible from afar.

Franz Kafka rented a room in the Schönborn Palace for a short period at the beginning of the 20th century.

Italian Lane `29`

[Vlašská] Ⓣ 12, 20, 22 MALOSTR. NÁMĚSTÍ

There were many Italians among the artists and craftsmen at the court of Emperor Rudolph II. They settled in the Lesser Town at the foot of Petřín Hill and eventually began building their own hospital and church in 1608.

In the second half of the 16th century, the gardens in the area of the marketplace [Tržiště] and John's Hill [Jánský vršek] were parcelled out and turned into building plots. The Italian Lane [Vlašská] and Mountain Lane [Břetislavova] were laid out at that time to provide access. Naturally, only very little of the former Italian character of the quarter remains today.

The **Hospital below Petřín Hill** [Vlašská 36–40] is a two-storey structure with four wings that originally served as a convent and

Italian Hospital at Vlašská.

Charles Borromeus' Church.

women's hospital. In 1851 the plain Charles Borromeus' Church in the Empire style was added. The hospital today forms a part of the Prague medical faculty.

The **Italian Hospital** [Vlašská 34] was a kind of charitable institution for the Italian community in Prague (masons, architects, master builders, painters); the hospital church was built between 1608 and 1617. The institution was closed down under the rule of Joseph II and the Italians subsequently turned it into an orphanage in 1804. The cartouche next to the main portal of the church shows the Good Samaritan.

During the Second World War, the so-called Casa d'Italia was set up on the premises of the Italian Hospital, the Italian Republic now maintains the Italian Cultural Institute here.

Lobkowicz Palace   30
[Lobkovický palác, Vlašská 19]
Ⓣ 12, 20, 22 MALOSTRANSKÉ NÁMĚSTÍ

This building was erected at the beginning of the 18th century to replace an earlier structure; in 1753 the high Baroque palace came into possession of the noble Bohemian Lobkowicz family. Its frontage seems cold and imposing, but the south-facing side of the Lobkowicz Palace merges gently with the garden, which looks towards Petřín Hill. In 1927, the Czechoslovakian Republic acquired the proud building and used it for administrative purposes. For a while, it

Lesser Town

Lobkowicz Palace (garden view).

Lobkowicz Palace (from the castle ramp).

served as the embassy of the People's Republic of China. Since 1973 it has been home to the diplomatic mission of the Federal Republic of Germany.

In autumn 1989, thousands of citizens of the GDR fled through the embassy of the FRG in Prague to the West. Thus, the Lobkowicz Palace became a site of historical importance for Germany in Prague. A Trabant car has been placed in the palace garden by a Czech artist, ironically set on tall legs, to commemorate this mass exodus. From the south balcony, which rests on columns, the then West German Minister for Foreign Affairs Hans-Dietrich Genscher announced to the jubilant refugees that there was no longer anything to stand in the way of their departure into the Federal Republic: "We have come here to inform you that today your departure has been made possible." A commemorative plaque on the wall reminds us of this historic moment.

St Lawrence's on Petřín Hill.

Petřín Hill 　31

[Petřín] Ⓣ 6, 9, 12, 20, 22 Újezd

Petřín Hill, 322 m high, is a moderate hill, popular for day trips, on the left bank of the Vltava, in the immediate neighbourhood of Castle Hill. A funicular leads up from Újezd to the plateau, but there is also a certain charm in approaching from behind, along the Italian Lane. There are quite a few objects of interest on the ridge of Petřín Hill – an observatory, a mirror maze [bludiště],

Observatory on Petřín Hill.

The Mácha Monument on Petřín Hill.

Observation tower on Petřín Hill.

St Lawrence's Church, magnificent rose gardens and a row of statues in honour of eminent personalities. The panoramic painting *The Battle against the Swedes on Prague Bridge in 1648* can be admired in its pavilion.

Probably the biggest attraction on Petřín Hill, however, is the 60 m high iron **observation tower**. Climbing the 299 steps is rewarded with a breathtaking view. This construction, erected in 1891, was inspired by the Eiffel Tower and demonstrates Prague's admiration for the *Grande Nation* and the city of Paris at the end of the 19th century.

Petřín Hill was also mentioned in his writings of Franz Kafka (especially in *Description of a Struggle*).

Church of Our Lady of Victory   `32`

[Chrám Panny Marie Vítězné, Karmelitská 9]   Ⓣ 12, 20, 22   HELLICHOVA

The church of the Lesser Town Germans was originally Protestant but received its present name after the Battle of White Mountain. At that time, the church was handed over to the Barefooted Carmelites, who were followed in 1784 by the order of St John of Jerusalem.

On a side-altar to the right is the gracious **Infant Jesus of Prague**. The wax figure dressed in valuable

Lesser Town

Façade of Our Lady of Victory.

101

The Infant Jesus of Prague.

the order of St John of Jerusalem ran a hospital here. The three-nave basilica belonging to this complex was largely expanded by the Maltese order in the 13th century. In 1420, in the course of the Hussite wars, the magnificent church was severely damaged; a conflagration in 1503 took care of the rest. The double portal beneath the characteristic Maltese cross leads to a kind of front garden and then to the church's Baroque interior, which was created by Carlo Lurago. The Czech Baroque artist Karel Škréta also contributed to its splendour. His work is visible in the altarpiece on the high altar (*The Assumption of the Holy Mary*) as well as in the paintings *The Beheading of St Barbara* and *The Victory at Lepanto*. A marble statue of 1857 commemorates Grand Prior Count Rudolf Colloredo-Wallsee who led the heroic defence of Prague against the Swedes in 1648 and whose last resting place is in front of the high altar.

robes originates from the 16th century and is said to work wonders. A Spanish princess brought it to Bohemia and her daughter, a princess Polyxena of Lobkowicz, gave it to the convent. In the pious Baroque age, the Infant Jesus of Prague was soon revered as having miraculous powers. Since then the holy site has been visited by pilgrims from all over the world.

Church of the Maltese Order of St Mary Below-the-Chain **33**

[Maltézský kostel „Panny Marie pod řetězem", Maltézské náměstí]
Ⓣ 12, 20, 22 HELLICHOVA

The foundations of the Church of the Maltese Order of St Mary Below-the-Chain can be traced back to the 12th century, when

Nostitz Palace **34**

[Nostický palác, Maltézské náměstí 1] Ⓣ 12, 20, 22 HELLICHOVA

The impressive four-winged palace was built for the aristocratic Nostitz-Rieneck family and sumptuously decorated. There are a few reminders of the earlier Renaissance period in this early Baroque building, but later alterations following the fashions of their day have also left their mark, such as the statues of the Prague high Baroque sculptors Ferdinand Maximilian Brokoff and Matthias Bernhard Braun, for example, or the Rococo decorations of around 1770, the portal by Anton Haffenecker, and the ornamental Empire-style balconies on the second floor that were added in the 19th century.

The Nostitz Palace houses a valuable 17th century library which consists of about 14,000 volumes.

The Grand Priory Square 35

[Velkopřevorské náměstí]
Ⓣ 12, 20, 22 HELLICHOVA

The extensive archives of the Maltese order and the order of St John of Jerusalem respectively are stored in the **Grand Priory building** [Velko-převorské náměstí 4]. The seat of the Grand Prior has been at the church since 1301.

The **Buquoy-Longueval Palace** [Vel-kopřevorské náměstí 2] was built in the second half of the 17th century on the orders of the Archbishop of Prague, Count Johann Friedrich von Wallenstein. Today, the French embassy is located in this palace.

Czechs (and especially tourists) come to the **John Lennon Wall** to commemorate their idol who set their hearts throbbing, especially in times of socialist restriction. Colourful graffiti make the wall a living, but – as it is painted over from time to time – transitory work of art.

Kampa Island 36

[Ostrov Kampa]
Ⓣ 6, 9, 12, 20, 22 ÚJEZD

Kampa Island is actually a peninsula which can be reached from the Lesser Town (as well as from Charles Bridge) and is situated between the Vltava and a creek called the "Devil's Stream" [Čer-tovka]. Despite its location, the Kampa area came under the jurisdiction of the Old Town. In medieval times it was a storage place for merchandise; over the course of the centuries, poor people, mostly washerwomen and raftsmen, settled down in the area which was liable to frequent flooding. Today Kampa Island is a tourist district with a small-town character and merges into a lively park to the south. Lovers of modern art would enjoy a visit to the Kampa Museum (formerly the Sova-Mills).

A particularly attractive part of the Kampa Island is known as "the Venice of Prague" because of the buildings right by the water. A famous pottery market was held on the island for centuries.

Lesser Town

Kampa Museum.

Row of houses on Kampa Island (Na Kampě).

The House "At the Three Ostriches"   **37**

[Dům „U Tří pštrosů",
Dražického náměstí 12]
Ⓣ 12, 20, 22 MALOSTRANSKÉ NÁMĚSTÍ

The fresco-adorned building on the Lesser Town end of Charles Bridge originates from the closing decades of the 16th century, while the two gables were added in the 17th century and are thus actually early Baroque. Prague's first coffee-house was established here by the Armenian Gorgos Hatalah el-Damaschi (Deodatus Damajan), who arrived from Damascus in around 1704.

St Joseph's Church   **38**

[Kostel sv. Josefa, Josefská]
Ⓣ 12, 20, 22 MALOSTRANSKÉ NÁMĚSTÍ

In the quiet Joseph's Lane close to the busy Bridge Lane stands a remarkable church. Its foundation was laid in 1673 in the presence of Emperor Leopold I, and

to this day the façade bears the coat of arms of the Habsburg monarch. Jean Baptiste Mathey, an influential figure in Prague as a master builder and imperial court architect, played an essential role in the design of the church with its elliptical ground plan. The shell was probably completed in 1690, but it took more than a decade longer to complete the interior.

The architecture itself combines with the furnishing and artistic decoration of the church to place it among the most treasured in Prague. The main painting on the Baroque altar is a portrait of the Holy Family and was executed by Peter Brandl in 1702. The picture of St Francis of Sales above it is a 19th century work by Josef Hellich. St Joseph's was to become the Church of the adjacent Carmelite Convent, the first in Prague. Towards the end of the 18th century it was however handed to the order of English Virgins, established by the Englishwoman Mary de Ward. Today, the English Virgins tend to the church once again. Sunday mass is also held in English here.

Idyllic scene on the Lesser Town bank of the Vltava.

Charles Bridge

[Karlův most]

The stone Charles Bridge.

On the "Stone Bridge"
[Karlův most]

Lesser Town Bridge Towers 39

[Malostranské mostecké věže]
Ⓣ 12, 20, 22 MALOSTRANSKÉ NÁMĚSTÍ

The smaller of the two towers dates back to the time of the Judith Bridge (second half of the 12th century), the first stone bridge to span the Vltava. Thus the tower is among the oldest buildings in town (the roof and its ornaments being 16th century alterations, however). The larger, late Gothic tower was only erected in 1464. It was intended as a companion for the Old Town bridge tower.

The gate complex is a special treat for heraldists, who will find here the historic city arms of the Old Town (three towers, city gate, half-raised grille; the armoured fist with the raised sword was only added after the Thirty Years' War), the city arms of the Lesser Town (also three towers, but with an opened gate and without a grille), as well as the coats of arms of the city of Wrocław and of Lower Lusatia, which formerly belonged to the Bohemian crown.

The castellated Gothic gateway could formerly be closed by a wrought-iron grille. Towards the bridge, right in front of the smaller bridge tower, is the former customs office, where the "Club for Old Prague", which has rendered outstanding service to the preservation of historic monuments, has been based since 1901.

Charles Bridge 40

[Karlův most, Praha 1]
Ⓣ 12, 20, 22 MALOSTRANSKÉ NÁMĚSTÍ

The Gothic Charles Bridge is considered to be one of the most important monuments of medieval architecture in Bohemia. There is thought to have been a ferry here as early as the 9th century, which was replaced with a wooden bridge by 1118, as the well-known Bohemian chronicler Cosmas informs us. The first stone bridge, the Judith Bridge, replaced the wooden construction in 1158. It stood firm and

Lesser Town bridge towers;
front left is the former customs office.

Charles Bridge

served Prague residents for almost two centuries until it was swept away by floods in 1342.

At exactly the time advised by his court astrologers – in the year 1357, on the 9th day of the 7th month, at 5:31 a.m. – Emperor Charles IV laid the foundation for the construction of the new bridge that would stretch over the Vltava with sixteen arches and be about 5 m higher than its predecessor. The architect and master builder Peter Parler came from Schwäbisch Gmünd, Swabia. The stone bridge remained the only connection between the Old Town of Prague and the Lesser Town until the 19th century.

Of the 30 **sculptures** on Charles Bridge, now mostly replaced by replicas, the most important is that of St Nepomuk. It was cast in Nuremberg in 1683, based on a model by Johann Brokoff.

Old Town Bridge Tower

41

[Staroměstská mostecká věž]
Ⓣ 17, 18 KARLOVY LÁZNĚ

At the same time as the construction of Charles Bridge in 1357, Peter Parler also built the Gothic defence tower on the Old Town bridgehead.

This tower was of great strategic importance in the defence of the Old Town (against the Swedes in the Thirty Years' War, for example). Fortunately, the bulwark survived the sometimes violent centuries relatively unharmed.

Dawn on Charles Bridge; the bronze statue of St Nepomuk on the far left.

Charles Bridge at night, Prague Castle in the background, St Nicholas' on the left.

Swedish shells however destroyed the figurative ornaments of the west façade. During repairs to the tower, the remnants were removed completely and replaced by the city arms of the Old Town. The coats of arms of countries that belonged to the dominion of Charles IV can be found on the eastern façade above the pointed arch. Beneath the row of heralic symbols is a kingfisher, the emblem of King Wenceslas IV. Above it, St Vitus the protector of the bridge stands on three piers and is flanked by the bridge's two royal patrons: Charles IV (left) and Wenceslas IV (right). On the top floor of the tower, the saints Adalbert and Sigismund have been placed above a sculpture of a (Bohemian) lion.

A spiral staircase winds its way up to the tower gallery and thus to a beautiful view over the roof-tops of the Old Town. A small passageway leads to the tower's formerly dreaded dungeon.

Old Town bridge tower (from the east).

Statues on Prague's Charles Bridge
(As seen from the Old Town bridgehead)

LEFT PARAPET
(As seen from the
Old Town bridgehead)

St Ivo, patron of advocates, 1711 by Matthias Bernhard Braun.

SS Barbara, Margaret and Elizabeth, 1707 by Ferdinand Maximilian Brokoff.

Pietà, 1859 by Emanuel Max. Here, the last Swedish onslaught towards the end of the Thirty Years' War (1648) was fended off with the help of students of Charles University (cf. the panoramic painting on Petřín Hill).

St Joseph, 1854 by Josef Max.

St Francis Xavier (the "Indian apostle"), 1711 by Ferdinand Maximilian Brokoff. The statue was badly damaged by the floods of 1890. The Jesuit Father Francis Xavier (1506–1552) did missionary work in East India and Japan among other places and earned his spot on the bridge for allegedly converting some 1.2 million pagans, whose various provenances are symbolised by the four kneeling figurines.

St Christopher, 1857 by Emanuel Max. A marble plaque on the bridge tower mentions that in the flood of 1784 a sentry post was washed away, together with the sentries, into the river here.

St Francis of Borgia, a Jesuit from Spain, 1710 by Ferdinand Maximilian Brokoff.

RIGHT PARAPET
(As seen from the
Old Town bridgehead)

St Bernard and the Mother of God, 1709 by Matthäus Wenzel Jäckel.

SS Mary, Dominic and Thomas Aquinus, 1708 by Matthäus Wenzel Jäckel.

Crucifix, 17th century. This bronze cross was cast by Hans Hillger in 1629 and was originally to adorn the bridge over the River Elbe in Dresden. In 1657 it was the first monument to be placed on Charles Bridge.
The Hebrew inscription was added only in 1696, paid for by a Jewish citizen as a fine for alleged blasphemy of the Holy Cross.

The Virgin and Child with St Anne, 1707 by Matthäus Wenzel Jäckel.

SS Cyril and Methodius with three allegories of Bohemia, Moravia and Slovakia, 1928–1938 by Karel Dvořák. This most recent group of statues replaced the previous statue of St Ignatius of Loyola.

St John the Baptist, 1757 by Josef Max. A marble plaque on the parapet designates the spot where John of Nepomuk was thrown into the Vltava in 1393 at the orders of King Wenceslas IV.

SS Norbert, Sigismund, and Wenceslas, 1853 by Josef Max.

St Ludmila. The statue of the first Christian duchess of the country was created in Matthias Bernhard Braun's workshop around 1730 and was transferred to the bridge from a church on Castle Hill in 1784.

St Franciscus Seraphicus (better known as Francis of Assisi), 1855 by Emanuel Max.

SS Vincenz Ferrerius and Procopius, 1712 by Ferdinand Maximilian Brokoff. Below the parapet stands the Roland Column (also called the Bruncvík statue), a knight with sword and shield that symbolises freedom of trade and the so-called "Stapelrecht", that is the right to unload goods and hold fairs.

St Nicholas Tolentinus, 1708 by Johann Friedrich Kohl.

St Luitgard with the Crucified Jesus, 1710 by Matthias Bernhard Braun based on a draft by Peter Brandl.

St Adalbert, national patron saint and Bishop of Prague, 1709 by Michael Josef Brokoff.

SS John of Matha, Ivan, Felix of Valois with the Turkish guards watching over Christian slaves, 1714 by Ferdinand Maximilian Brokoff. John of Matha and Felix of Valois were the founders of the Trinitarian order, which was established in 1198 to ransom Christian captives. St Ivan on the other hand – easily recognisable by the full beard and long hair – is considered to have been the first Bohemian hermit.

St Wenceslas, Bohemian national patron saint, 1858 by Josef Kamil Böhm. The Bohemian Duke Wenceslas (about 903–929), grandson of St Ludmila, actively promoted the Christianisation of Bohemia and pushed the country towards its integration into the Holy Roman Empire. This stirred up a pagan-nationalist reaction, under the leadership of his brother Boleslav I, who eventually assassinated him. The anniversary of St Wenceslas' death (28th September) is a public holiday.

St John of Nepomuk, Vicar General of the Archbishopric of Prague. Bronze statue cast by Wolfgang Hieronymus Heroldt in Nuremberg in 1683 based on models by Johann Brokoff and Matthias Rauchmüller. John of Nepomuk is revered as the martyr of the seal of the confessional since he is said to have refused to divulge to King Wenceslas IV the confession of his queen.

St Antony of Padua, 1707 by Johann Ulrich Mayer, a sculptor probably from Vienna, granted citizenship of the Lesser Town of Prague in 1712.

St Jude Thaddeus, apostle, 1708 by Johann Ulrich Mayer.

St Augustine, father of the Latin Church, 1708 by Johann Friedrich Kohl.

St Cajetan with angels, 1709 by Ferdinand Maximilian Brokoff.

St Philip Benitius, c. 1711 by Michael Bernhard Mändl. The area beneath the statue is known as the "Venice of Prague".

St Vitus on a cliff with lions, patron saint of the Prague Bridge, 1714 by Ferdinand Maximilian Brokoff.

SS Cosmas and Damian, patron saints of physicians and apothecaries, 1709 by Johann Ulrich Mayer.

The Virgin and Child with St Anne.

The Old Town

[Staré Město]

A Walk through the Old Town
[Staré Město]

The first of the four historical cities of Prague, the Old Town, nestles in a semi-circular bend of the river, affording it ideal protection. Its beginnings go back to the first millenium of the Christian calendar, although there was obviously no reason to name the small market town "Old Town" at the time. This term only came into use after Charles IV founded the "New Town" in the 14th century. The Prague Jewish Quarter developed in the northwest of the Old Town area, directly bordering the banks of the River Vltava.

The centre of the Old Town consists of the Old Town Square dominted by the City Hall and Týn Church.

Another significant centre developed around St Gallus' Church [kostel sv. Havla]: the Gallus Town.

In the course of the Emperor Joseph II's administrative reforms, the Prague cities (i.e. the Castle District, the Lesser Town, New Town and Old Town) were united in 1784. From then on, the City Hall of Prague was located at the Old Town Square.

In the 20th century the Old Town of Prague underwent drastic changes which have robbed the area of a lot of its original charm. The redevelopment of the Prague Jewish Quarter (about 1900) is one example, as are the politically motivated removal of the Marian column that used to be in front of the City Hall (in 1918) and the destruction of the east wing of the neo-Gothic City Hall during the Prague uprisings in May 1945. Despite many losses, the Old Town Square is considered one of the most beautiful architectural ensembles in Europe today.

Impressive townhouses on the north of Old Town Square.

Old Town Square

42

[Staroměstské náměstí]
Ⓜ A, B Můstek or Ⓜ A Staroměstská

If Wenceslas Square in the New Town is a point of culmination in recent national history, then the walls of the Old Town Square mirror the events of many centuries past that have left their mark in eminent buildings. The square is actually neither square nor rectangular, in fact, the ground plan is extremely irregular. The Romanesque, Gothic, Renaissance and Baroque styles combine to form a unique composition, rightly perceived as the centre of the historical city of Prague.

As well as important monuments, palaces, and churches there are proud townhouses whose history dates back to medieval times.

House "At the Minute",
one of the Kafka sites in Prague.

The family of the writer Franz Kafka lived in the house **"At the Minute"** [Staroměstské náměstí 2] between July 1889 and September 1896. Kafka's three sisters Elli, Valli and Ottla were born here. This building has an early 17th century sgraffito façade (which, however, was painted over in Kafka's time). The lion guarding the corner was the trademark of the pharmacy formerly situated here, named **"At the White Lion"**.

The house **"At the Golden Angels"** [Staroměstské náměstí 29] is home to the famous restaurant **"At the Prince"**, where German poet Detlev von Liliencron was a regular during his visits to Prague. The statue of St Florian is from the 18th century.

The wine and ale tavern "Binder" ("Barrel-Cooper"), where the German painter Carl Spitzweg tippled in 1849, was located in the house **"At the Blue Goose"** [Staroměstské náměstí 25].

The house **"At the Golden Unicorn"** [Staroměstské náměstí 20] was Czech poet Karel Havlíček Borovský's home in the years 1838–39. Later, Bedřich Smetana ran a music school here.

The apothecary's wife, Berta Fanta, organized a literary salon in the house **"At the Unicorn Pharmacy"** [Staroměstské náměstí 17] that was frequented by personalities like Franz Kafka, Max Brod and Albert Einstein.

The **"Štorch House"** [Staroměstské náměstí 16], built in the so-called Vladislavistic Gothic style, is renowned for its painted façade based on designs by the Czech painter Mikoláš Aleš (*Portrayal of St Wenceslas*). The name of the building commemorates its builder, the Prague publisher Alexander Štorch (his German surname meaning "Ostrich").

The **"Oppelt House"** [Staroměstské náměstí 3] was one of Franz Kafka's adresses after November 1913. Among other pieces, he wrote his short stories *The Judgement* and *The Metamorphosis* here.

Old Town

117

Old Town City Hall   **43**

[Staroměstská radnice, Staroměstské náměstí 3]   Ⓜ A, B Můstek

After King John of Luxembourg had sanctioned the construction of a City Hall in 1338, the citizens of the Old Town of Prague used the income from a wine tax to purchase a private townhouse on the Old Town Square. A council chamber was founded and an apartment for the town clerk was furnished, as well as cells built for convicts. The Gothic **City Hall tower** was added in 1364 and was the first of its kind in medieval Prague. The **St Andrew's Chapel** on the second floor was consecrated in 1381, during the reign of Wenceslas IV. The original City Hall was destroyed in a fire in 1399 and was rebuilt in 1407. In the 19th century a remarkable change was made to the ensemble by the addition of the elegant neo-Gothic north wing.

During the heavy fighting in May 1945 the neo-Gothic north wing and the east wing of the Prague City Hall were destroyed. Fortunately, the tower remained intact. The famous Astronomical Clock of 1410 was successfully set in motion again after the Second World War.

The **Astronomical Clock** mirrors a medieval view of the world: The planets revolve around the earth, not the sun. Every day at midnight, a clock hand moves ahead to indicate the new day. Figurines of the Saviour and the twelve apostles are paraded at the hour. After all the disciples have passed, a golden cockerel crows in the tympanum. Beneath it to the right, death sways his hourglass and rings the death knell.

The tower of the Old Town Hall.

The Astronomical Clock at the City Hall.

Renaissance window on the façade of the Old Town Hall.

The man standing next to the dial on the left can't redeem himself from his destiny despite his bulging moneybag; death shakes his head at such desperate attempts of bribery. There are also allegories of vanity, greed and paganism. Archangel Michael with shield and sword warns of the Last Judgement. In 1866, a dial with medallions for the twelve months (painted by Josef Mánes) was added to the decorative clock ["orloj" in Czech, derived from the Latin "Horologium"].

A late Gothic gateway next to the Astronomical Clock is the entrance to the City Hall. On the second floor, the late Gothic **council chamber** awaits visitors with a painted Renaissance beam ceiling, the city arms, a crucifix, and several dozen guild signs. The new **assembly hall** was built in 1879 and was decorated with impressive historical paintings by Václav Brožík: *The Election of George of Poděbrady as King of Bohemia* (an event which took place in the Old Town City Hall in 1458) and *Jan Hus before the Council of Constance.* Equally worth a visit – and open to the public free of charge – is the **vestibule** with mosaics based on works by the Czech painter Mikoláš Aleš (including *Libuše predicts Prague's fame*).

119

The adjoining Renaissance wing to the left, with the extraordinarily beautiful tripartite window, the inscription PRAGA CAPUT REGNI and the Prague city arms, is also part of the City Hall.

Today the Old Town City Hall merely serves prestigious purposes. As such, it is probably the nation's most sought-after venue for weddings.

The pillory and the place of execution stood in front of the Town Hall from the Middle Ages on. Every Czech history schoolbook mentions an execution which took place here on 21st June 1621: 27 Protestant rebels (Germans and Czechs), including the Rector of Charles University, Dr. medicinae Johann Jesenius, were executed on the scaffold beneath the bay chapel. 27 crosses on the pavement in front of the City Hall commemorate this act of retribution after the Battle of White Mountain.

St Nicholas' Church in the Old Town.

The Church of St Nicholas in the Old Town 44

[Kostel sv. Mikuláše na Starém Městě, Staroměstské náměstí] Ⓜ A STAROMĚSTSKÁ

The splendid Baroque St Nicholas' Church was built in 1732–1737 right next to the (former) Jewish Quarter. It is the work of the great Kilian Ignaz Dientzenhofer.

The figurative ornaments on the façade were created by Anton Braun, a nephew of Matthias Bernhard Braun. Benedict and Norbert, who both founded monastic orders, flank the south portal; set in the niches are the holy physicians Cosmas and Damian. Inside the church is a magnificent chandelier from Harrachov, a Bohemian Town in the Giant Mountains [Krkonoše], as well as a large fresco in the octagonal dome, the theme of which is the legend of St Nicholas.

In the course of the Josephine Reforms the church was deconsecrated in 1787 and turned into a warehouse. Almost a century later, in 1874, the church was equipped for Russian Orthodox services. After the First World War, St Nicholas in the Old Town became the main church of the Czechoslovakian Hussites.

Kinsky Palace 45

[Palác Kinských, Staroměstské náměstí 12] Ⓜ A, B MŮSTEK

This proud Baroque palace is a late work of Kilian Ignaz Dientzenhofer, completed by Anselmo Lurago (1755–1765). The sculptures on its fascia come from

Kinsky Palace (left) and the house "At the Stone Bell" (right).

Ignaz Franz Platzer's workshop. The Empire-style staircase made in 1835–1836 is also noteworthy. The palace was initially built for Johann Arnold von Goltz. In 1786 it came into possession of the Kinsky family, who were expropriated after the Second World War as a result of the notorious Beneš decrees. Today this building with its unique rococo façade, protruding far into the Old Town Square, belongs to the National Gallery.

Bertha von Suttner (author of *Lay Down Your Arms!*, 1889), born 1843 and later to win the Nobel Peace Prize, spent her early childhood in the Kinsky Palace.

From September 1893, Franz Kafka attended the German humanist state grammar school, situated in the palace courtyard, eventually passing his matriculation exams in September 1901.

The haberdasher's shop owned by Kafka's father was later to move into the same building. Today, there is a bookshop on the premises which commemorates the great Prague writer.

On 21st February 1948 the communist Prime Minister Klement Gottwald stood on the balcony of the Kinsky Palace to announce the dismissal of all conservative ministers; as a result, Czechoslovakia became a communist nation.

House "At the Stone Bell" 46

[Dům „U Kamenného zvonu", Staroměstské nám. 13] Ⓜ A, B MŮSTEK

This three-storey tower was built on the foundations of an early Gothic townhouse in the second half of the 13th century. A chapel

Old Town

121

was added in a second period of construction around 1310; it was richly adorned with figurines and ornaments, of which unfortunately only fragments have remained. The characteristic house symbol on the corner, the stone bell, was affixed in the 16th century. Baroque alterations after 1685, as well as those of the 18th and 19th centuries, considerably changed the appearance of the building. After extensive research and reconstruction work, the building has now more or less regained its original late medieval appearance. Presently the halls of the house "At the Stone Bell" are used as venues for concerts and exhibitions.

Church of Our Lady before Týn   **47**

[Chrám Matky Boží před Týnem, Staroměstské nám.] Ⓜ A, B Můstek

The Church of Our Lady before Týn was founded by traders and merchants in the mid 14th century. The construction work was carried out by Peter Parler's cathedral stonemasons. The 80 m high towers, each with eight pointed spires, are a landmark amid the maze of roofs in the Old Town.

The arcade of buildings in front of the church, restricting what can be seen of it, housed the famous "Týn School" as far back as the Middle Ages.

Construction work had to be stopped during the Hussite unrest. Later, the elected King George of Poděbrady had the church and its two distinctive towers completed. It became the Hussites' main church between 1419 and 1621. A statue of George of Poděbrady, portrayed as the protector of the Hussite chalice with a drawn sword, was placed on the gabled roof. It was removed soon after the victory of the Catholic Habsburgs at the Battle of White Mountain, and the gilded chalice was melted down to form the halo of the Madonna which now occupies the tympanum.

Inside the church is the marble tomb of the famous Danish astronomer Tycho de Brahe. He was summoned to Prague in 1599 by Emperor Rudolph II. The life-size relief figure is dressed in full armour.

Among the treasures of the lavishly decorated church are several panels by the Czech Baroque painter Karel

The spires of Týn Church.

Škréta (*The Angelic Salutation* on the altar of the annunciation, or *The Assumption* on the high altar, for example), a statue of the Slavic apostles Cyril and Methodius made of Carrara marble, a large wooden crucifix from the time of Charles IV, a late Gothic stone baldachin by Matthias Rejsek over the grave of the Italian suffragan bishop Augustinus Lucianus de Mirandola, a 15th century Gothic pulpit, a carved altar with a portrayal of the baptism of Christ, a pewter font in the shape of an inverted bell bearing a relief of the apostles, the Lady of Týn, carved from limewood, and a High Baroque oval relief of the Holy Family (below the organ loft).

Prague writer Franz Kafka.

Birthplace of the writer Franz Kafka 49

[nám. Franze Kafky 5]
Ⓜ A STAROMĚSTSKÁ

Old Town

Franz Kafka was born on the 3rd July 1883 as the first of the six children of the haberdasher Hermann Kafka and his wife Julie. His birthplace on the north end of the Old Town Square bordered the Prague ghetto, still in existence at that time, in the immediate vicinity of the Baroque St Nicholas' Church. The house was built between 1717 and 1730 by Kilian Ignaz Dientzenhofer to accommodate the Prelate of St Nicholas in the Old Town. After the dissolution of the monastery in 1787 under Emperor Joseph II, it was converted into a residential house.

After it burned down in 1897, a tenement house was erected in its place; the doorway of the original

Monument of Jan Hus.

Jan Hus Monument 48

[Pomník Jana Husa, Staroměstské náměstí] Ⓜ A, B MŮSTEK

Somewhat too large for the dimensions of the square, this monument by Ladislav Šaloun was unveiled on 6th July 1915, the 500th anniversary of the reformer Jan Hus' death at the stake. Hus stands upright looking towards the Týn Church, which had been at least temporarily the Hussite Bishop's Church.

Franz Kafka's birthplace.

building is all that remains of Kafka's birthplace. There is now a small Kafka exhibition on the premises.

It was not until 1965 that a commemorative bust was installed on the façade; seventy-six years after the death of probably Prague's most famous son, the square in front of his birthplace was renamed 'Franz Kafka Square'.

Canvas Makers' Lane   50

[Celetná, Praha 1]
Ⓜ B NÁMĚSTÍ REPUBLIKY

The promenade and shopping street leading from the Old Town Square to Republic Square forms part of the so-called "Royal Path". Participants in the ceremonial coronation processions took this route from the Royal Court in the Old Town to St Vitus' Cathedral, the coronation church. In less stable times, the Bohemian kings returned to the fortified Prague Castle and the Royal Path lost its significance.

Such illustrious personalities as Cola da Rienzi, Francesco Petrarca or Jo-

hann Faust were guests at the **"Sixt House"** [Celetná 2]. In the 17th century it belonged to the scribe Phillipus Fabricius, who was thrust out of the window of the old chancellery in 1618. He survived the Defenestration and was ennobled and given the title "von Hohenfall" (of the High Fall). As a child, Franz Kafka also lived in this building from 1888–1889.

Kafka lived in the house **"At the Three Kings"** [Celetná 3] as an adolescent.

The house **"At the White Lion"** [Celetná 6] is adorned with an original house symbol.

Mozart's hostess in Prague, the pharmacist's daughter Josepha Dušková, hailed from the house **"At the Black Sun"** [Celetná 8].

The house **"At the White Peacock"** [Celetná 10] has an impressive Rococo façade and an original house symbol.

Hermann Kafka's shop was temporarily located at the **Hrzán-of-Harasov Palace** [Celetná 12]. The palace is thought to have been built according to plans by Giovanni Alliprandi.

The originally Romanesque **Caretto-Millesimo Palace** [Celetná 13] was remodelled in the Baroque style in around 1756; it has a particularly beautiful Baroque doorway.

The Canvas Makers' Lane.

House symbol "At the Golden Angel".

writer Theodor Fontane, working as a war correspondent at the time.

The **Pachta Palace** [Celetná 36] was originally a mint and became Prague's military headquarters in 1784. During the Prague Whitsun revolt of 1848, the first gunfights between the revolutionaries and troops of the Prague military Commandant General Windischgrätz broke out in front of this building. Since 1850 it has served as a courthouse and Franz Kafka was among those who have worked here. The figurative decoration was created by Ignaz Franz Platzer.

The house **"At the Vulture"** [Celetná 22] originally housed a brewery. Since the 18th century it has been one of Charles University's lecture halls. A gilt inscription over the Baroque doorway is a reminder of the "k.u.k. [Imperial and Royal] Privileged Factory of Gold Articles, Prokop Hindle & Son", formerly located here. After 1861, the building was also home to the Mercy printing plant, the head office of the famous *Prager Tagblatt* newspaper and the editorial department of the *Prager Morgenpost*.

The **"Manhart House"** [Celetná 17] was once a Piarist College; it bears a Baroque statue of St Nepomuk on the façade above the first storey.

The house **"At the Red Eagle"** [Celetná 21] boasts a particularly beautiful house symbol.

The house **"At the Bohemian Eagle"** [Celetná 30] is an 1897 tenement house in the style of the Czech neo-Renaissance.

The house **"At the Black Madonna"** [Celetná 34] was built by Josef Gočár in 1911–12. It was the first Cubist building in Europe.

The philosopher and theologian Bernard Bolzano lived and died in the house **"At the Four Columns"** [Celetná 25].

There was formerly a church and a hospital on the site of the house **"At the Temple"** [Celetná 27]

The house **"At the Golden Angel"** [Celetná 29] used to be a hotel; the revolutionary Michail Bakunin stayed here in 1848 as did later the German

Powder Tower · 51

[Prašná brána, Celetná, Praha 1]
Ⓜ B NÁMĚSTÍ REPUBLIKY

In 1475, a 65 m high tower was erected to replace the dilapidated 13th century Kutná Hora Gate, which straddled the road to the silver-mining town of Kutná Hora. The Rector of the Týn School, Master Matthias Rejsek, oversaw the construction works. The name of the tower refers to

Old Town

The Gothic Powder Tower.

the gunpowder stored there from time to time. It was connected to the neighbouring Royal Court by a wooden bridge. The tower was badly damaged by Prussian shells in 1757. It was not until the 19th century that the tower was finally completed in the neo-Gothic style by cathedral master builder Josef Mocker.

Two lavishly decorated halls can be visited in the interior of the Powder Tower.

Representation House 52
[Obecní dům, náměstí Republiky 5]
Ⓜ B Náměstí Republiky

The prestigious Representation House was built in the so-called Prague Secessionist style in the years 1906–1912 on the site of the former Royal Court. The "Repre", as the locals like to call it, is the venue of choice for prestigious balls, concerts (particularly in the Smetana Hall), meetings, and similar occasions. There is a historic café as well as an elegant restaurant on the ground floor.

The architects Osvald Polívka and Antonín Balšánek strove for a decidedly romantic nationalist note (adding relief medallions depicting traditional costumes, for example). The mosaic *Homage to Prague* is a work by Karel Špillar. Ladislav Šaloun contributed two beautiful groups of statues – symbolising the humiliation and resurrection of the people. The Secessionist painter Alfons Mucha is represented by valuable allegorical paintings in the "Mayor's Hall". The Czechoslovakian Republic was proclaimed in the Representation House on October 28th 1918, and, in 1989, a round table was held here, at which the commun-

Mosaic on the Representation House: Libuše predicts the fame of the city of Prague.

ist leadership negotiated with the opposition under the chairmanship of Václav Havel.

St Jacob's Church `53`

[Kostel sv. Jakuba, Malá Štupartská]
Ⓜ B NÁMĚSTÍ REPUBLIKY

This church, the exterior of which is decorated with stucco reliefs by Ottavio Mosto (1695), was the minster of a Minorite monastery founded by Wenceslas I. Only fragments of the monastery buildings remain. The three-nave basilica was completed in 1374. Its Baroque décor was created in the first half of the 18th century. The altarpiece on the high altar depicts the martyrdom of St Jacob and is a 1739 work of the Bohemian Baroque painter Wenzel Lorenz Reiner. In a side chapel is the almost 9 m high tomb created by Johann Bernhard Fischer von Erlach and Ferdinand Maximilian Brokoff for the Bohemian Chancellor, Count Johann Wenzel Vratislav of Mitrowicz (died 1712).

Thanks to its good organ and excellent acoustics, concerts and musical high masses are held in the church. The Czech musician Bohuslav Czernohorský served as organist here.

Týn Courtyard `54`
["Ungelt"]

[Týnský dvůr] Ⓜ B NÁMĚSTÍ REPUBLIKY

The main building of the complex known as the Týn Courtyard is the "Ungelt", where the legendary customs collector Jakob von Granov officiated. This Renaissance palace with an open loggia on the first floor (as well as 16th century murals and sgraffitos depicting biblical and mythological scenes) served as a hostel for foreign traders. Inscribed above the doorway are the Granov family's coat of arms and the date 1560. The complex burned to the ground in a conflagration in the 17th century and townhouses were afterwards built on the site of the old customs court.

The German term "Ungelt" – "Geld" meaning money – is a reminder of the medieval purpose of the ducal customs court. Here travelling traders were to pay storage and customs charges for all goods that would pass through Bohemia.
Only within the Týn Courtyard were they permitted to trade goods, where they had to avail themselves of the brokerage of civil servants, which, naturally, didn't come without handling charges.

In the Týn Courtyard ["Ungelt"].

Old Town

Karolinum 55
[Karolinum, Železná/Ovocný trh]
Ⓜ A, B MŮSTEK

The famous Charles University, the first university north of the Alps, founded on April 7th 1348 by the Emperor Charles IV, moved in 1383 into the former premises of the royal master minter Johann Rotlöw, the pres-ent-day Karolinum. However, only a magnificent Gothic bay window – part of the Chapel of Saints Cosmas and Damian (around 1370) – an arcade and the assembly hall on the second floor, where academic ceremonies are held to this day, remain of the beginnings of this venerable institution. Since its early days, Charles University has also held up a mirror to Bohemian national history.

After its short-lived heyday at the beginning of the 15th century, the Kuttenberg decree of 1409 resulted in the decline of the university. With the decree, King Wenceslas IV gave in to Rector Jan Hus's demand for a Bohemian majority in the university's administration.

The "natio bohemica", which included both the German and the Czech sons of the Bohemian crown lands, now had three votes as opposed to the Bavarian, Saxon and Polish members of the university, who had to content themselves with just one. This caused large numbers of students, university teachers and professors to leave Charles University for other institutes (Krakow, Heidelberg, Vienna, Cologne; a new university was even specifically founded in Leipzig). Until 1622, when it was taken over by the Jesuits, Charles University had a reputation in the Christian world as a breeding ground for heretics.

In the 19th and 20th centuries, the venerable institution was, once again, the scene of fierce national and political clashes. In 1882 the university was divided into two mutually independent Czech and German universities. The

The Karolinum's Gothic bay window.

Czech University was closed down on 17th November 1939 at the orders of the Reichsprotektor; President Edvard Beneš avenged this act by retroactively closing down the German University in 1945. Charles University was to play a significant part in the nation's political history on two further occasions: during the months of the so-called Prague Spring in 1967–68, and in 1989, when the student body played a vital role in the "Velvet Revolution" exactly 50 years after the closure of the Czech University.

Estates' Theatre **56**

[Stavovské divadlo, Ovocný trh 1]
Ⓜ A, B Můstek

This classicist theatre was originally named Nostitz Theatre after its builder Count Franz Anton Nostitz-Rieneck. He had it built between 1781 and 1783 right next to Charles University – much

Estates' Theatre in the Old Town.

to the regret of the teaching staff, who feared that the students would be all too distracted from their studies by the presence of a theatre. Premieres of famous operas were held at the Estates' Theatre, such as Mozart's *Don Giovanni* (1787) and *La clemenza di Tito* (1791) for example. Many world-renowned artists have given guest performances here, such as Niccolò Paganini, Clara Schumann, Richard Wagner or Carl Maria von Weber, who was its director in 1813–16. Shorty before the theatre was closed for upcoming renovations in 1983, it served as the setting for *Amadeus*, Miloš Forman's film about Mozart.

St Gallus' Church **57**

[Kostel sv. Havla, Havelská]
Ⓜ A, B Můstek

This church has a beautifully curving Baroque façade; its name, along with that of the surrounding area, comes from the skull of St Gallus bought from St Gallen, Switzerland, in the Middle Ages. Innumerable pilgrims came to Prague to see the relic – until it was lost during the Hussite wars. Eminent theologians and preachers have officiated in St Gallus' Church, including Jan Hus and John of Nepomuk.
Karel Škréta, one of the most important Czech Baroque painters, has found his last resting-place here.
The quarter around the church is known as Gallus Town and

Old Town

129

dates back to medieval times. The Gothic arcades of the charming Gallus' Lane [Havelská] are a reminder of the period in which a large number of German townsmen lived here. Today the stalls of the street market that has been held here since 1232 convey at least some of the atmosphere of a medieval market place.

House "At the Two Golden Bears" 58

[Dům „U Dvou zlatých medvědů", Kožná 1] Ⓜ A, B MŮSTEK

At the junction of Leather Lane [Kožná ulička] and Melantrich Lane [Melantrichova] is an eye-catching building with a Renaissance doorway and a conspicuous house symbol (two bears). It is the birthplace of the "Racing Reporter" Egon Erwin Kisch (1885–1948). Kisch is one of the German-speaking Prague writers who became famous beyond the country's borders along with Franz Kafka, Max Brod, Rainer Maria Rilke and Franz Werfel.

Coal Market 59

[Uhelný trh] Ⓜ A, B MŮSTEK

A graceful Empire-style fountain of 1797, with figures made by Franz Xaver Lederer, adorns the coal market. Locals also call it the Wimmer fountain after the surname of its donor. The square itself derives its name from an old smithy with a charcoal kiln that stood here until the early 19th century. Legend has it that

this smithy was one of Dr Faustus' lodgings in Prague.

Wolfgang Amadeus Mozart stayed **"At the Three Lions"** [Uhelný trh 1] in 1787. From here, it was just a short walk for the "Kapellmeister" to the Estates' Theatre and the rehearsals of his opera *Don Giovanni*.

The house **"At the Cancasters"** [Uhelný trh 6] is the former editorial department of the newspaper *Prager Postzeitung*.

The house **"At the Two Cats"** [Uhelný trh 10] is a well-known Pilsner beer-house. In the 19th century a famous piano shop, in which a young Antonín Dvořák gave his first public performance, was located here

The Hungarian composer Franz Liszt lived in the **"Platýz"** [Uhelný trh 11] between 1840 and 1846. As Prague's primary tenement house, it was said to yield handsome returns and thus went by the name "At the Golden Hen" among locals.

Church of "St Martin in the Wall" 60

[Kostel sv. Martina ve zdi, Martinská 8] Ⓜ B NÁRODNÍ TŘÍDA

The Gothic parish church of "St Martin in the Wall" at the former city walls is now used by the evangelical Bohemian Brethren. St Martin's Cemetery formerly belonged to the church; the Bohemian Baroque sculptor Ferdinand Maximilian Brokoff (1688–1731) is buried here along with his family – a memorial plaque commemorates the fact.

This church gained historical significance for the Hussite movement in 1414 as the first to administer the Eucharist in both kinds (bread and wine), "sub utraque specie", and to the entire congregation. As the issue of "wine" was not the least divisive, the chalice became the symbol of the Hussite revolution. The Utraquists (or Calixtines, after the Latin "calix" for chalice) read mass in Czech until the counter-reformation – this was also one of the central demands of the Hussite reformers.

Bethlehem Chapel 61
[Betlémská kaple, Betlémské náměstí] Ⓜ B Národní třída

In this chapel, founded in 1391, Master Jan Hus, the Rector of Prague University, began in 1402 to hold fiery speeches against the deficiencies of church organisation and the decline of moral standards. Thus the Bethlehem Chapel is of great symbolic

significance. In 1521 the German reformer Thomas Müntzer preached here. After the Thirty Years' War the Jesuits, summoned to Prague to revive Catholicism, tried to get rid of the Bethlehem Chapel along with all memories of the wretched "spirit of heresy" that pervaded it. Eventually, the national shrine was demolished in 1786. In the 1950s the Bethlehem Chapel was reconstructed on the historic remnants.

Little Square 62
[Malé náměstí] Ⓜ A, B Můstek

This idyllic square was the pharmacist's district in centuries past. A beautiful 16th century fountain, vaulted by an artful wrought-iron grille, stands in the centre of the square. Since 1650, a gilt

Old Town

Bethlehem Chapel
on Bethlehem Square.

The Bohemian lion
on the fountain at the Little Square.

Bohemian lion has adorned the top of the fountain grille.

The **House of the Judge** [Malé náměstí 11] was the oldest pharmacy in Prague.

The house **"At the Golden Lily"** [Malé náměstí 12] is also a former pharmacy. The plain Baroque townhouse of 1698 is the only documented place of residence of architect and master builder Christoph Dientzenhofer.

To this day there is a pharmacy in the house **"At the Golden Crown"** [Malé náměstí 13].

Angelus of Florence, the court pharmacist of Charles IV, worked in the house **"At the Angel"** [Malé náměstí 1].

The house **"At the White Lion"** [Malé náměstí 2] has a Gothic doorway with a heraldic lion on the spandrel as well as a Rococo relief of the resurrection of Christ.

The **Rott House** [Malé náměstí 3] has impressive historic murals based on sketches by Mikoláš Aleš. The first Bible in Czech was printed here in 1488.

Marian Square   63
[Mariánské nám.]   Ⓜ A STAROMĚSTSKÁ

The peculiar architectural charm of the Marian Square is often overlooked by hasty visitors, as the modern square is surrounded by palatial buildings that immediately attract attention to themselves. Amid the towering palaces though is the pleasant detail of the statue of the Vltava on the fountain in the garden wall of the Clam-Gallas Palace. The allegory was created by Wenzel Prachner (1812), the most influential representative of Prague Classicism, and is affectionately known as "Terezka" by locals.

The **Prague Municipal Library** [Mariánské nám. 1] is a 1920s palace built by František Roith in the style of representative Functionalism. Here the Mayor, called Primator in Prague, has a prestigious apartment.

Townhouses at the Little Square.

The New City Hall at Marian Square.

A popular puppet theatre has also found a home in this building.

The **New City Hall** [Mariánské náměstí 2], a splendid art nouveau building, is the official residence of the Mayor of Prague. There are two statues of legendary figures by Ladislav Šaloun conspicuously placed at the building's corners: *The Black Knight* and *Rabbi Loew*.

Clam-Gallas Palace 64

[Clam-Gallasův palác, Husova 20]
Ⓜ A STAROMĚSTSKÁ

The Clam-Gallas Palace is one of the chief works of Baroque architecture in Prague, a collaboration of eminent contemporary architects, sculptors and painters resulting in a harmonic ensemble of masterly secular architecture. The Viennese Imperial court architect, Johann Bernhard Fischer von Erlach, drew up the plans in person in 1713; their execution was placed in the hands of an Italian – Domenico Canevale. Matthias Bernhard Braun contributed the two pairs of giants guarding the doorways. A ceiling fresco by Carlo Carlone,

Old Town

Rabbi Loew at the New City Hall.

Façade of the Clam-Gallas Palace.

133

Staircase of the Clam-Gallas Palace.

the *Triumph of Apollo* can be admired above arguably the most beautiful staircase in the city, The Clam-Gallas Palace was the stately home of the Country Marshall of Bohemia, Count Johann Wenzel von Gallas, the pin-

Atlases at the Clam-Gallas Palace.

nacle of whose diplomatic career was his appointment as Viceroy of Naples. Today, the Municipal Archive of Prague administers a large inventory of vedutas, engravings, old maps, photographs, certificates, signets etc. here.

Dominican Church of St Aegidius 65

[Dominikánský kostel sv. Jiljí, Jilská]
Ⓜ B NÁRODNÍ TŘÍDA

A choirless hall church with nave and side aisles of equal height built prior to 1370, St Aegidius' Church holds a special place in the sacred architecture of Prague. It fell victim to a great fire in 1432 and consequently had to be rebuilt. Some 200 years later, in 1626, the Dominicans took over the church and had the early Baroque monastery added by Carlo Lurago. The church's interior was likewise given a Baroque makeover. The plans for this were probably provided by Kilian Ignaz Dientzenhofer. Wenzel Lorenz Reiner (1689–1743), Bohemia's most important Baroque painter, is buried inthe Dominican church's righthand side aisle. Reiner also created some of the frescoes in the church interior (nave: *Triumph of the Dominicans over the Heretics*; side aisle: *St Wenceslas*). The main altarpiece by Friedrich Johann Hess depicts the foundation of the Dominican order. The country's first music conservatory was located here in the 19th century.

Rotunda of the Holy Cross 66

[Rotunda sv. Kříže, Karoliny Světlé]
Ⓣ 6, 9, 17, 18, 21, 22 NÁRODNÍ DIVADLO

The Romanesque Rotunda of the Holy Cross was built in the early 12th century and was closed in 1784. A group of artists intervened to prevent the demolition of this Romanesque gem in the 19th century. It was restored at that time, uncovering 14th century Gothic murals in the process. The iron grille around the chapel was designed by the Czech painter Josef Mánes.

Rotunda of the Holy Cross.

Smetana Museum on the Novotný Footbridge 67

[Smetanovo muzeum, Novotného lávka 2] Ⓣ 17, 18 KARLOVY LÁZNĚ

This 1885 neo-Renaissance building served as the office of the Municipal Waterworks Department until the 1930s. Bedřich Smetana had lived in the nearby Lažanský Palace on the Vltava from 1868 to 1869, composing his famous opera *The Bartered Bride* there; thus in 1936, a museum dedicated to the Czech composer was set up in the former Waterworks' office on the Novotný Footbridge. Here there is a display of manuscripts and exhibits from the maestro's personal estate.

In 1984 a monument to the composer was put up in front of the Smetana Museum.

Old Town

Novotný Footbridge on the Old Town embankment; the Smetana Museum to the left.

Knights of the Cross Square.

Knights of the Cross Square

68

[Křižovnické náměstí, Praha 1]
Ⓣ 17, 18 KARLOVY LÁZNĚ

The Old Town bridge tower, probably the most beautiful bridge tower in Europe; the statue of Emperor Charles IV; St Salvator's Church with the Clementinum; the Church of the Knights of the Cross; a marvellous view of the River Vltava, Prague Castle, the Lesser Town and the Old Town spires – all this combines to make the **Square of the Knights of the Cross** one of the most magnificent in Prague. Locals sometimes refer to it as their "parlour"; an affectionate description that scarcely evokes the thundering traffic and crowds of tourists.

A statue of Emperor Charles IV presides over the square. Charles is holding the charter of the Prague University he founded; beneath him are allegories of the four traditional faculties as well as representations of eminent contemporaries of the Luxembourgian monarch, among them Matthew of Arras, the first master builder of St Vitus' Cathedral. The monument was cast in Nuremberg and was to be unveiled on the occasion of the 500th Jubilee of Charles University, but the revolutionary turmoil of 1848 meant that the ceremony had to be postponed until 1849.

At the Church of the Knights of the Cross, on the corner facing the street, stands a Baroque "winegrowers column" by Johann Georg Bendl. The monument consists of a statue of St Wenceslas on a column entwined with vine leaves and was commissioned by the City Council of Prague in 1676. It originally stood in front of the Department of Viniculture at the end of the Charles Bridge. Eventually, it had to make way for the increased traffic and was thus moved to its current position. 13th century cobblestones from the medieval road

Statue of Charles IV.

leading to the Judith Bridge, then still in existence, can be seen around its base. They were uncovered in 1910 in the course of sewer construction works and preserved for posterity.

The Church of the Knights of the Cross [69]

[Kostel sv. Františka Serafínského, Křižovnické náměstí]
Ⓣ 17, 18 Karlovy lázně

The monastery church of the highly regarded "Knights of the Cross with a Red Star", the only knightly order to be founded in Bohemia, was built in imitation of St Peter's Basilica in Rome and, like its model, its magnificent dome is particularly impressive. The façade with figures of angels and saints, including a statue of St Nepomuk by Richard

Church of the Knights of the Cross.

Prachner, was designed by Jean Baptiste Mathey, thus bringing a piece of French Classicism to the Vltava. In the interior, we encounter once again the art of Bohemian Baroque painter Wenzel Lorenz Reiner. The master craftsman adorned the oval dome with a depiction of the Last Judgement and the spandrel with the four Church Fathers.

After 1252, the Knights of the Cross lived according to the rule of St Augustine at the Old Town bridge head of Charles Bridge. They were in charge of the maintenance of the old Judith Bridge and collected customs and bridge tolls. This proved to be a steady source of income for the thriving and wealthy order, untouched even by the Hussite turmoil.
The Knights of the Cross were famous for fostering church music. Willibald Gluck and Antonín Dvořák were among the organists here. Karl Postl (1783–1864), a Knight of the Cross from the region of Znojmo, was to become an important American author under the name of Charles Sealsfield after his flight from the monastery.

Clementinum [70]

[Klementinum, Křižovnická/Karlova/ Platnéřská] Ⓣ 17, 18 Karlovy lázně

The former Jesuit College spreads over five courtyards and at least three churches belong to it: **St Salvator's**; **St Clemens'**, built to the plans of Kilian Ignaz Dientzenhofer and which in 1560 displayed the first nativity scene in the country; and the **Italian Chapel**, noteworthy for its elliptical ground plan and which served the Italian congregation. Today the Clementinum

Old Town

137

The *Prague Student* in the Clementinum.

The friars took over the former Dominican monastery, devastated during the Hussite wars, and made it the headquarters of the counter-reformation. A Catholic university (since 1616), the Clementinum was intended to be the antithesis to Charles University with its Protestant tendencies, although the latter was also taken by the Jesuits after the victory at White Mountain. In 1653, soon after the 30 Years' War, they laid the foundation stone for the campus of the Clementinum as we know it today. Emperor Ferdinand III contributed most of the costs of the ambitious project, which had an enormous political impact in its time. Its dimensions speak for themselves: after Prague Castle, the Clementinum is the largest complex of buildings in the historic city.

houses both the University Library and the National Library. The splendid **Mirror Chapel** is a venue for classical concerts. Emperor Ferdinand I summoned the Jesuits to Prague in 1556.

The Clementinum.

The Jesuits were driven out of Prague several times; nonetheless, they were ultimately able to assert themselves on the Vltava. However, their Golden Age didn't last forever: the rule of reformist Emperor Joseph II spelled the end of the Jesuits era – the friars had to leave Prague and the Clementinum became an archiepiscopal seminary and thus an exclusive school for future priests.

A monument commemorating the defence of Prague by students in 1648, made by the brothers Emanuel and Josef Calasanca Max, has been set up in one of the Clementinum's courtyards.

acteristic tripartite triumphal arc was built in the late 16th century in the Renaissance style. After Baroque extensions in the 17th century, the spires were added in 1714.

The statues on the balustrade and on the gable (1659) are by Johann Georg Bendl. The stucco decoration of the interior and the images of the twelve apostles on the confessionals are also by Bendl.

The Jesuit historian Bohuslav Balbín who died in 1688 is buried in the crypt.

The Church of St Salvator **71**

[Kostel sv. Salvátora, Karlova]
Ⓣ 17, 18 KARLOVY LÁZNĚ

Forming part of the Clementinum, this church with its char-

Charles' Lane **72**

[Karlova] Ⓣ 17, 18 KARLOVY LÁZNĚ

The lane connecting Charles Bridge and the Old Town Square, formerly known as "Jesuits' Lane", is nowadays one of the

Old Town

The busy Charles' Lane.

busiest streets in Prague. Despite the crowds among the shops, there are a couple of historically significant buildings that should not be overlooked.

The "Winter King", Frederick of the Palatinate, is believed to have fled from the **Colloredo-Mansfeld Palace** [Karlova 2] after losing the Battle of White Mountain in 1621. In the courtyard there is a beautiful Neptune fountain.

The astronomer Johannes Kepler lived and worked in the house **"At the French Crown"** [Karlova 4] between 1607 and 1612.

The wealthy Schönfeld family of publishers, printers and book dealers resided in the **Schönfeld Palace** [Karlova 12].

House "At the Golden Well".

Prague's first coffee brewer Deodatus Damajan of Damascus had an apartment in the Renaissance house **"At the Golden Snake"** [Karlova 18].

The first cinema in Prague, the so-called "Biograph Ponrepo", opened its doors in the tenement house **"At the Blue Pike"** [Karlova 20].

The house **"At the Golden Well"** [Karlova 3] was formerly the papal Nunciature. It boasts magnificent Baroque façade with figurative reliefs by Johann Ulrich Meyer dating from 1701: a reproduction of a medallion of the Virgin Mary of Stará Boleslav who is surrounded by the Bohemian saints Wenceslas and John of Nepomuk as well as the "plague saints" Roch and Sebastian. The tympanum shows the plague saint Rosalia lying in her grave.

Decoration of a
Charles' Lane shop.

St Salvator's Church 73

[Kostel U Salvátora, Salvátorská]
Ⓜ A STAROMĚSTSKÁ

This single-vessel hall church was built before the Thirty Years' War with the help of Protestant Christians from all over Europe and served the Lutherans of the Old Town. After the Battle of White Mountain it fell to the Pauline Order; the Protestant preachers had to leave Prague. After the dissolution of the Pauline monastery in the Josephine period, the church was temporarily used as a mint. Since 1918 it has been the main church of the Bohemian Brethren.

The Church of the Holy Ghost   74
[Kostel sv. Ducha, Elišky Krásnohorské] Ⓜ A STAROMĚSTSKÁ

This Gothic church was built in 1346 and originally belonged to a Benedictine monastery destroyed by the Hussites in 1420. The church itself survived the Hussite wars but fell victim to the conflagration of 1689. In the course of its reconstruction it was furnished with a Baroque vault. A simple statue of St Nepomuk by Ferdinand Maximilian Brokoff stands in front of the Church of the Holy Ghost.

Hospitallers' Monastery   75
[Klášter U Pavlánů, U Milosrdných 1] Ⓣ 5, 8, 14 DLOUHÁ

There has been a hospital in this location since as early as the closing decades of the Middle Ages. The protestant Bohemian Brethren eventually erected a single-vessel church in the early 17th century, which was handed to the Hospitallers after the Battle of White Mountain.

Local legend has it that a wooden staircase inside the hospital was made from the same planks and beams previously used in the scaffold on which the 27 Bohemian noblemen were executed on the Old Town Square. The Church of SS Simon and Jude, belongs to the monastery; the altarpiece was painted by Wenzel Lorenz Reiner.

As it has excellent acoustics, the Gothic church is nowadays used for concerts. Joseph Haydn and Wolfgang Amadeus Mozart are said to have played on its organ (which is decorated with figures by Johann Brokoff).

St Agnes' Convent   76
[Anežský klášter, U Milosrdných 17] Ⓣ 5, 8, 14 DLOUHÁ

The construction of this large convent began in 1234 at the special request of the devout Princess Agnes, daughter of the Bohemian King Přemysl Otakar I. At its peak, it comprised seven churches and two cloisters. St Agnes' Convent was granted to the Franciscan order and divided into a monastery for brothers of the Minorite order and a convent for nuns of the order of St Clare. The founder Agnes herself joined the latter order, along with seven other noble ladies, and became its abbess from 1235–1237.

Princess Agnes, canonised in 1989, had corresponded with St Clare and even during her lifetime she was known for her

Old Town

St Agnes' Convent.

that of the convent founder, Princess Agnes, was found during the restoration of St Salvator's Church; King Wenceslas I lies buried in St Francis' Church. Finding the remains of Princess Agnes was of great symbolic significance, as an old prophecy said: "When once the body of the blessed Agnes is found in Prague, war and unrest will cease in Bohemia and a Golden Age will dawn over the land".

Today St Agnes' Convent is home to collections of medieval Bohemian and Central European art belonging to the National Gallery, which are well worth seeing.

humble and abstemious lifestyle. Not even Emperor Frederick II could convince her to trade the crown of her virginity for the Imperial one.

The convent was deserted during the Hussite unrest, yet the centuries that followed brought a regular monastic lifestyle back to the institution. However, in 1782, it was among the convents dissolved by Emperor Joseph II. By the end of the 19th century, the buildings had lain waste for such a long time that complete demolition was considered.

Extensive restorations, still continuing to this day, have ensured the continued existence of this important monument of Bohemian Gothic architecture. A cloister, the chapter hall and the refectory survive from the time of the foundation of the convent, and are open to the public.

Two of the churches in the complex contain important graves:

St Castulus' Square and Church   **77**

[Haštalské náměstí a kostel sv. Haštala] Ⓣ 5, 8, 14 DLOUHÁ

A 14th century basilica dominates this peaceful square in the Old Town. Originally it had three aisles; however in 1375 the northern nave was replaced by a remarkable double-aisled hall; thus the church is now a four-aisle basilica. The church arches over dainty columns decorated with masks and a pattern of plants. A spire rises over the southern aisle. A fire burned the church to the ground in 1689; the reconstruction that followed was executed in a partly Baroque manner.

The interior decoration includes a Baroque calvary group by Ferdinand Maximilian Brokoff from 1716 and Gothic murals that have been preserved in the vestry.

The Jewish Quarter
[Židovské město]

A Tour of the Prague Jewish Quarter

[Pražské židovské město]

No one can say for certain when the Jews came to Bohemia, or where, and in what numbers, they settled down; the origins are obscure. Early medieval records show that Jewish traders, physicians and civil servants were already living in Prague at that time. At least two Jewish settlements can be proved to have existed in the 10th and 11th centuries, one below Prague Castle and another at Vyšehrad. After the year 1100, the Jewish community settled in the area of the Spanish Synagogue. The famous Prague Jewish Quarter, the walled ghetto in the Old Town, gradually developed towards the end of the 12th century.

The Jews of Prague had a time of considerable properity under the rule of Rudolph II, when Mordechai Maisel, the wealthy mayor of the Jewish Town and the Emperor's court financier, had the ghetto lanes paved, provided for orphaned brides, had synagogues, schools, baths and the famous City Hall built, and had the Jewish Cemetery "Beth-Chajim" (House of Life) laid out. The esteemed Rabbi Loew worked and taught in the Prague Jewish Quarter around the same time – he was to go down in history not only as an important cabbalist and theologian but also as the creator of the Golem, central to many legends. According to them, Rabbi Loew's creation helped the Jews in times of persecution.

At Easter 1389, the ghetto experienced one of the cruellest pogroms in the history of Prague Jewry. The walls of the Old-New Synagogue are said to have been stained red by the blood of those killed.

The entire Jewish community was driven out twice: in 1541 under Emperor Ferdinand I and in 1744 under the rule of Maria Theresia, who decreed the expulsion of all Jews from Bohemia. Three years after the last families had left, the monarch

found herself forced to revoke the expulsion decree. It was not until an edict of toleration was issued by her son Joseph II that the Jews' situation improved. The Jewish Quarter, which is now called Josefov in honour of the reforming Emperor, soon fell into disrepair, however, as affluent families moved away into better parts of the city. Low dives, poverty and prostitution soon became characteristic of the Josefov.

After countless meetings and resolutions, a radical clean-up was implemented around 1890; unfortunately a large part of the historical fabric was also ruined in the process. The twisty dark lanes of the poor were replaced by modern Art Nouveau palaces of rich citizens and industrialists. A wide boulevard, the Paris Street [Pařížská] was laid out – even today, it remains one of the grandest streets in the city.

The National Socialists eventually dealt the death blow to the Jewish community. Almost 80,000 Jews from the Reich Protectorate of Bohemia-Moravia lost their lives in the years of occupation between 1939 and 1945.

The Jewish Museum, founded in 1906, houses a unique collection of diverse artefacts and documents. It is spread out over many buildings and synagogues. The Jewish Museum is closed on Saturdays for the Sabbath – as are all other institutions in the Jewish Quarter.

Maisel Synagogue 78

[Maiselova synagoga, Maiselova 10] Ⓜ A STAROMĚSTSKÁ

This synagogue is one of those founded by Mordechai Maisel and, in its time, it was considered to be the most magnificent building in the Jewish Quarter. Its main hall is supported by 20 columns and was built by Josef Wahl and Juda Goldschmied in around 1590 in the Renaissance style.

The temple was damaged by the great fire of 1689 and was subsequently reconstructed in the Baroque manner. At the turn of the 20th century the synagogue was refashioned in the neo-Gothic style. During the time of the Protectorate, the temple served as the storehouse for confiscated furniture and articles from the houses and flats of displaced Jews. The synagogue is currently displaying

The Maisel Synagogue.

silver from Bohemian synagogues as well as an exibition on the history of Bohemian and Moravian Jews.

The Jewish City Hall   **79**
[Židovská radnice, Maiselova 18]   Ⓜ A STAROMĚSTSKÁ

The Jewish City Hall was built by the Italian architect Pankraz Roder in the 1680s in close proximity to the Old-New Synagogue. Once again, the rich primate Mordechai Maisel financed the building.

The City Hall is the seat of the council of the Jewish community of Prague and houses a ritual dining hall as well as municipal offices. The Jewish Museum with its unique collection of ritual textiles (curtains from synagogues across Europe, Torah coats etc) has also found a home under its roof.

After the Swedish siege of 1648, the Jews were permitted to construct a belfry as a reward for their service in the defence of the town. In 1763 the City Hall was reconstructed and fitted with a rococo façade as well as a wooden extension to the belfry. Two clocks tell the time: the one on the belfry has a Latin dial, the other, on the roof of the City Hall, has Hebrew numbers that read from right to the left like the Hebrew script.

The **City Hall Synagogue** next to the City Hall itself is also known as the "High Synagogue" [Vysoká synagoga], because the prayer room, an elegant late

The clock of the Old Jewish City Hall.

Renaissance hall, is on the second floor.

The Old-New Synagogue 80

[Staronová synagoga,
Červená] Ⓜ A STAROMĚSTSKÁ

This temple is the oldest synagogue in Europe still serving its original purpose. It was built around 1270 by the royal stonemasons' lodge. In the early 14th century the entrance hall was added; later, the two counters for tax officials were inserted here. Another 14th century work is the decoration of the tympanum above the portal, which shows Israel as a grapevine with the twelve tribes as its roots.

The characteristic brick gables not added until the 15th century. Subsequently, in the 18th century, the synagogue was extended to include the side aisle with small windows to allow Jewish women to watch the service in the main prayer hall. An orthodox Jewish woman was only allowed to enter into the holy area of the synagogue once in her life: on her wedding day.

A few steps lead down to the synagogue proper, which is divided into two aisles by two octagonal pillars. In the centre of the room is the Almemor, a kind of lectern from which the Torah is read and addresses are delivered to the congregation. An iron grille surrounds the altar room with its large nine-armed candelabrum. Fitted into the eastern wall and framed by Renaissance

columns is the Torah shrine, where the parchment scrolls with the five books of Moses are stored. Above it is another tympanum relief of vine leaves and tendrils.

Columns support the cross vault which has five radials, thus differentiating itself from the Cross of Christ, the symbol of Christianity, and its four radials.

The Banner of Prague Jewry (Shield of David and Jewish hat) dates back to a gift of Emperor Charles IV, who in 1357 granted the Jewish community of Prague the privilege of a flag of its own. Many eminent rabbis have been heads of the synagogue, such as Jehuda ben Bezalel (Rabbi Loew) or Solomon Judah Löb Rapoport, one of the pioneers of scientific Jewish Studies.

The Old-New Synagogue.

Jewish Quarter

The Former Ceremonial Hall
of the Jewish Quarter.

The Former Ceremonial Hall   81

[Obřadní síň, U Starého hřbitova 3a]
Ⓜ A STAROMĚSTSKÁ

The neo-Romanesque building, which was built of ashlar blocks at the entrance to the Old Jewish Cemetery in 1908, is home to an exhibition on death and disease: Texts and illustrations document the work of the Funeral Brethren and explain Jewish rituals like the cleaning of the corpses and various burial ceremonies. A separate room is dedicated to Jewish cemeteries and tombstones.

The Old Jewish Cemetery "Beth Chaim"   82

[Starý židovský hřbitov, Široká]
Ⓜ A STAROMĚSTSKÁ

The Old Jewish Cemetery in Prague is the second oldest Jewish graveyard in Europe, after the Jewish cemetery in Worms. The oldest gravestone at the cemetery (from 1439) commemorates Avigdor Ben Isaak Kara, who chronicled the Easter pogroms of 1389. There are thought to be about 20,000 gravestones, layered on top of each other, in these 11,000m² grounds; in the course of centuries, the dead have been buried on top of each other in up to twelve layers. Pictorial depiction of the dead is forbidden in the Jewish faith, therefore carp, foxes, lions, bears, lancets, books, axes, cans and suchlike adorn the gravestones, giving information about the names, occupations or origins of those buried there.

Visitors often leave little notes at the graves of the better-known personalities, on which they have written various wishes, weighing them down with little stones. The grave of the rich Primate of the Jewish Quarter, Mordechai Maisel, (died 1601), and the Renaissance tomb of the great Rabbi Jehuda Loew Ben Bezalel (died 1609) are among the most

interesting. Also remarkable are the graves of the astronomer, physician and philosopher Josef del Medigo (died 1655), the scholar David Gans and Hendl Baschewi, wife of Jakob Baschewi "von Treuenburg", the magnate and first Bohemian Jew to be raised to nobility.

The last burial took place in 1787. Burials within the city walls were forbidden at that time for reasons of hygiene. The New Jewish Cemetery in Strašnice, established in those days, has been the last resting place of the Jews of Prague ever since. During the "sanitation" of the Jewish Quarter, part of the Old Jewish Cemetery was levelled.

At the Old Jewish Cemetery.

"Klausen" Synagogue   **83**

[Klausová synagoga, U Starého hřbitova]   Ⓜ A STAROMĚSTSKÁ

Rabbi Jehuda Loew lived and worked as a teacher of the Talmud in this plain synagogue, which was built on the premises of the Old Jewish Cemetery and donated by Mordechai Maisel. The synagogue originally consisted of three smaller buildings (called "Klausen" in German) that burned down in 1689. Their name however survived and was conferred on the new building (built 1694 to 1696). The "Klausen" Synagogue was also the meeting place of the Jewish Funeral Brethren of Prague. Today it is used by the Jewish Museum to exhibit items related to Jewish traditions and customs.

The Pinkas' Synagogue   **84**

[Pinkasova synagoga, Široká]   Ⓜ A STAROMĚSTSKÁ

Pinkas' Synagogue was built on the site of a synagogue dating back to the 11th century, which thus could well have been the oldest synagogue in Prague. In the 14th century, the land belonged to a certain Rabbi Pinkas, who consequently gave his name to the synagogue built here in 1535. Around 1625, the Pinkas' Synagogue was reconstructed in the style of late Renaissance and was extended to include a conference hall and a women's gallery. In the 1950s, the Pinkas' Synagogue was turned into a memorial

Jewish Quarter

151

The Pinkas Synagogue.

The Spanish Synagogue.

to the victims of the Nazi rule: the names of 77,297 murdered Jews from the Reich Protectorate of Bohemia-Moravia were identified on the basis of deportation files. The names were listed alphabetically by place of origin and family name on the walls of the nave and the adjoining rooms.

cember 2003 on what would have been Kafka's 120th birthday. The 700 kg bronze statue by the Czech sculptor Jaroslav Róna shows the poet "riding" on the shoulders of a male figure who has been reduced to a mere shell.

Spanish Synagogue 85
[Španělská synagoga, Vězeňská 1]
Ⓜ A Staroměstská

In 1882, a historicised domed central structure was built on the site of the "Altschul" (Old School), perhaps Prague's oldest synagogue, burned down in 1389 and eventually replaced by a new synagogue in 1605. This was the synagogue for Jews living according to eastern rites. The building is inspired by the Spanish Alhambra. The gilt stuccowork in the interior and the Moorish appearance of the temple were intended to commemorate the Jews driven out of Spain who had found temporary refuge in Prague.

Close to the Spanish Synagogue, a 3.75 m high monument to Franz Kafka was unveiled in De-

Franz Kafka monument in Prague.

Arts-and-Crafts Museum 86

[Uměleckoprůmyslové muzeum, 17. listopadu 2] Ⓜ A STAROMĚSTSKÁ

Built by Josef Schulz and commissioned in 1901, the museum houses the world's largest collection of glass as well as masterpieces of furniture and metalwork, ceramics, textiles etc. The museum is situated with-in the historic Prague Jewish Quarter.

House of Artists Rudolfinum 87

[Dům umělců, náměstí Jana Palacha 1] Ⓜ A STAROMĚSTSKÁ

The concert hall, built in 1880 by the architects Josef Zítek and Josef Schulz in the prestigeous neo-Renaissance style, gets its name from the unfortunate crown prince, Rudolph of Habsburg. Between 1918 and 1939 the Czechoslovakian National Assembly held its debates in this magnificent building; today the Rudolfinum is once again at the service of the muses under the name of the "House of Artists". Regular concerts by, among others, the Czech Philharmonic Orchestra are held here and it is the base of the famous "Prague Spring" music festival. Sculptures of important composers such as Wolfgang Amadeus Mozart and Felix Mendelssohn-Bartholdy can be seen on the balustrade.

Next to the Rudolfinum is a monument made by Bohumil Kafka in 1951 and dedicated to the Czech painter Josef Mánes, whose name the nearby Mánes Bridge (1911), leading to the Lesser Town, also bears. In front of the building a statue of the Czech composer Antonín Dvořák looks up at what must be the most splendid concert hall in the Czech Republic.

Jewish Quarter

The Rudolfinum concert hall.

The New Town

[Nové Město]

A Tour of the New Town
[Nové Město]

The New Town, established by Charles IV more than 650 years ago in 1348, on the site of older settlements, is no longer true to its name. Of course, it is still virginal in comparison to the Old Town or Prague Castle, the origins of which go back to the first millenium AD.

The city of Prague was bursting at the seams, so by founding the New Town, Emperor Charles IV gave it further scope for development. He not only determined the course of the streets and squares but also dictated the location of the churches, which were all to be made of stone. His medieval development and traffic planning were able to cope with all the technical demands of transportation until the 20th century.

In a very real sense, the New Town has maintained, or rather developed, a very youthful and lively atmosphere even today. Modern city life unfolds here, important firms have branches here, and, above all, this is where great political and cultural manifestations and revolutions took place, particularly in the 20th century. Today the New Town, with Wenceslas Square at its centre, is expensive and luxurious, ruled by chic and elegance. There are no reminders that it was once the poorer population who eked out an existence here, providing a fertile breeding ground for the revolutionary Hussite movement. Thus, the Hussite turmoil started in the Prague New Town, in the course of which, this part of the town also suffered extensive damage.

The middle-class residential area of "Royal Vineyards" [Vinohrady] is also known as the **"Upper New Town"**, here, the wealth of the "Gründerzeit" (1874–1914) is still evident.

Two churches are well worth visiting: the **Archdeaconry Church of St Ludmila**, built by the cathedral master builder Josef Mocker 1888–1893, and the **Sacred Heart** at George of Poděbrady Square [náměstí Jiřího z Poděbrad] designed between 1928 and 1932 by the Slovene architect Josip Plečnik.

Wenceslas Square   88
[Václavské náměstí]
Ⓜ A, B Můstek or Ⓜ A, C Muzeum

The square extends from Můstek, which borders the Old Town, up to the former Horse Gate, now the site of the National Museum. At the beginning of the 19th century, the largest boulevard of Prague (750 m in length, 60 m wide) was still surrounded by buildings from one to three storeys in height; it only took on its current metropolitan character in the 20th century. On the broad pavements of the shopping street, flanked by avenues of lime trees, young Prague meets tourists from all over the world. The opinion of the German poet Detlev von Liliencron, who called Wenceslas Square the "world's proudest boulevard", holds true to this day. Until 1848 it was known as the "Horse Market" because of the annual equestrian market held here. The Czech journalist and author Karel Havlíček Borovský suggested renaming the boulevard Wenceslas Square in 1848, the year of revolutions. This was intended to commemorate the revolutionary meetings held at the beginning of the June revolution of 1848 in the so-called "Wenceslas' Baths" that were situated here. The Czechoslovakian Republic was proclaimed on the 28th October at Wenceslas Square, which slopes upwards towards the National Museum. Similarly, masses gathered here in May 1945, 1968 and 1989, in part to watch the political changes of each era, in part to drive them along.

After the First World War, the Art Nouveau Palace **"Koruna"** [Václavské náměstí 1] boasted an automated buffet, which was very modern in its day and would offer a meal for a single crown. The 1912 palace however owes its name not to the machine, but to the splendid crown on its turret. The building that preceded the "Koruna" was home to the Café "Edison", where the American inventor was a customer during his stay in Prague.

The **Hotel Ambassador** [Václavské náměstí 5] is a prime example of Prague Art Nouveau.

The **Baťa Building** [Václavské náměstí 6] is a functionalist building, built for the Moravian shoe manufacturer Baťa in 1928–29. The reinforced concrete construction is seven storeys tall and has a glazed façade facing the Square; in its day, it was considered to rank among the most modern department stores in Europe. A passage leads through to Jungmann Square.

"At the Golden Goose" [Zlatá husa, Václavské náměstí 7] is an exclusive hotel with a proud history.

The **"Café Praha"** [Václavské náměstí 10] is a Constructivist coffee-house built in 1929 and mentioned in Max Brod's social novels.

Franz Kafka began his career as an insurance clerk in the **"Assicurazioni Generali"** Palace [Václavské náměstí 19].

Koruna Palace at Wenceslas Square.

157

Hotel Adria [Václavské náměstí 26] is a late Baroque building erected in 1789.

The **Wiehl House** [Václavské náměstí 34] was built by Antonín Wiehl in 1895–96 in a neo-Renaissance style. The adornments on the façade are based on sketches by Mikoláš Aleš and Josef Fanta and had to be restored after serious damage suffered in 1945.

Václav Havel and Alexandr Dubček held speeches from the Palace **"Melantrich"** [Václavské náměstí 36] during the "Velvet Revolution" (1989).

The **Lucerna Palace** [Václavské náměstí 38] was built by Václav Havel's grandfather during the First World War. It was the first reinforced concrete construction in town and has been a centre of Prague's social life and a favourite venue for balls ever since it opened its doors.

The 1906 Art Nouveau **Grandhotel Evropa** [Václavské náměstí 27] has an elegant café. Here Franz Kafka gave a public reading from his short story *The Judgement* in 1912.

St Wenceslas monument.

St Wenceslas Monument 89

[Pomník sv. Václava, Václavské náměstí] Ⓜ A, C Muzeum

In 1912, a monumental equestrian statue of St Wenceslas, the patron saint of Bohemia, was erected in upper Wenceslas Square to replace an earlier Baroque version by Johann Georg Bendl, transferred to Vyšehrad in 1879. Surrounding the saint's horse are larger-than-life statues of Saints Ludmila, Agnes, Procopius and Adalbert. The Czech sculptor Josef Václav Myslbek is said to have spent 30 years working on the monument.

Various memorable events in national political history are closely linked to the statue of St Wenceslas on his steed. Locals are fond of "their horse", however, because they know the spot "under the tail" as a place for chivalrous trysts and romantic rendezvous. Even "babička" (grandmother) stood here as a girl with a throbbing heart and … a mind far from politics!

National Museum 90

[Národní muzeum, Václavské náměstí 68] Ⓜ A, C Muzeum

The museum, over 70 m high and with a frontage length of 100 m, was built by Josef Schulz between 1885 and 1890 in the neo-

Renaissance style. The mighty domed edifice built in place of the former Horse Gate is of great symbolic value to the Czech nation.

The main front with its statue-adorned ramp is a striking sight: next to Bohemia on her throne are a young girl, embodying the Vltava, and an old man, personifying the River Elbe. The fountain figures are flanked by allegories of Moravia and Silesia. Bohemia is depicted once again in the tympanum, this time as a patron of the arts and sciences Grouped around the dome are allegorical statues by Bohuslav Schnirch (Willingness to Make Sacrifices, Enthusiasm, Love of Truth and History).

On the first floor is the history section; the department for nat-

In the National Museum.

ural sciences is on the second floor. The National Museum Library is one the most important in the country, holding almost a million volumes including valuable medieval manuscripts. Also of great value are the mineralogical-geological collections of the French geologist Joachim Barrande.

Wenceslas Square and the National Museum at night.

New Town

State Opera (formerly New German Theatre) `91`

[Státní opera, Wilsonova 4, Praha 1]
Ⓜ A, C Muzeum

After 1859, there was a wooden construction on this site: the "New Town Theatre", where performances were staged in the summer months. Until 1882, this makeshift theatre was directed by no less a figure than Bedřich Smetana.

A few years later, the present neo-Rococo opera house was built according to the plans of the busy Vienna-based theatre architects Hermann Helmer and Ferdinand Fellner. The chariot of Dionysus and the muse Thalia are portrayed on the pediment of the Classicist façade. Until the end of the Second World War, busts of Mozart, Goethe and Schiller stood immediately below them.

The building was erected on behalf of the German Theatre Association, impressed by the Czech theatre-mania, and financed by private donations and collections. The grand opening was celebrated on the 5th January 1888 with a performance of Richard Wagner's *The Mastersingers of Nuremberg*, and soon this stage became a stepping stone into the German-speaking world for Austrian and Bohemian actors.

The opera director Angelo Neumann, who had been called to the banks of the Vltava from Bremen, was very well able to create a German theatre of national significance in a city that was, by then, predominantly Czech.

Central Station `92`

[Hlavní nádraží, Wilsonova]
Ⓜ C Hlavní nádraží

The central station, originally named after Emperor Francis Joseph, was built from 1901–1909 based on a design by the Czech architect Josef Fanta. The four stone towers in the style of the Prague Secession lend it a distinctive appearance.

The green tree-lined space in front of the central station is a remnant of what was once the city park, named after Jaroslav Vrchlický. Town planning measures in the 1970s robbed it of the particular charm that it must have had around 1900. A plaque on the building at no. 41 Ople-

The State Opera.

Prague Central Station.

talova, put up by the Austrian Society for Literature, commemorates Franz Werfel, who used to live in this area by the city park.

St Henry's Church 93

[Kostel sv. Jindřicha, Jindřišská]
Ⓣ 3, 9, 14, 24 JINDŘIŠSKÁ

The parish church in the Upper New Town, commissioned by Emperor Charles IV, was intended to have a double tower, but only one was built. Set apart in a small garden, once the graveyard, stands the church's belfry with the "Maria" bell, which was cast by master Bartholomew in 1518. The former defence tower was severely damaged during the Swedish siege of 1648.

The three-nave church, which was regothicized along with the belfry in 1875–1879 by Josef Mocker, has sandstone statues of St John of Nepomuk and Judas Thaddeus by Michael Josef Brokoff; the altar piece depicts the patron of the church, Emperor Henry II, with his wife St Cunigund and is a work of Johann Georg Heintsch. Two paintings by Wenzel Lorenz Reiner are to be found in the Chapel of Our Lady of Sorrows.

Old Customs Office "At the Hibernians" 94

[U Hybernů, náměstí Republiky 3]
Ⓜ B NÁMĚSTÍ REPUBLIKY

In 1625, Irish Franciscan monks (the Latin word for Ireland being Hibernia) who were expelled from their homeland during the reign of Queen Elizabeth I, came to Prague and found refuge in a Benedictine monastery which had been established in 1359. Here

New Town

they reconstructed **St Ambrosius' Church** which had been destroyed in the Hussite wars. By the time the former Baroque church received its splendid Empire-style façade (1808–1811), the Hibernian monastery was already secularised. The building has since served as a tobacco depot and the main customs office; since the 1940s it has been an exhibition centre and trade fair hall.

The old customs office "At the Hibernians".

"In the Moat" 95

[Na Příkopě] Ⓜ A, B Můstek

The present shopping street and promenade between the Powder Tower [Prašná brána] and Můstek, at the lower end of Wenceslas Square, derives its name from the moat, which until 1816, separated the Old Town from the New Town.

The **Czech National Bank** [Na Příkopě 28] was built in 1938 on the site of two well-established hotels, the "Blue Star" and the "Black Horse". Such prominent guests as

A view of the "Moat".

Hector Berlioz, Richard Wagner, Fyodor Dostoevsky and Carl Spitzweg had stayed here. Kaiser Wilhelm and Prince Bismarck signed the Peace of Prague at the "Blue Star" hotel on August 23rd 1866.

The former **"German House at the Moat"** was renamed "Slavic House" [Slovanský dům] in 1945. Originally a Baroque palace, it was remodelled in the Classicist style and had served as the social centre of the Prague Germans since 1873. Several German societies held their meetings here. Famous poets such as Detlev von Liliencron, Rainer Maria Rilke and Gerhard Hauptmann read from their works in the Mirror Hall of the "German House". On a visit to Prague, her native city, in 1895, the dedicated pacifist Bertha von Suttner delivered a speech in the "German House".

The former **Palace of the Landbank** [Na Příkopě 20] is richly decorated with statues and mosaics. It was built on the site of the Nostitz Palace, where the Prague Slavic Congress was held in 1848.

Eminent personalities such as Bernard Bolzano, Franz Werfel, Max Brod, Rainer Maria Rilke and Karel Hynek Mácha graced the benches of the **Piarist Grammar School** [Na Příkopě 16].

The **Church of the Holy Cross** was built from 1816–1824 and belonged to a former Piarist convent. Its two Ionic columns rank it as a perfect example of the Empire style.

There is a plaque at the **ČSOB Bank** [Na Příkopě 14] to commemorate Božena Němcová. The Czech poetess died on the 21st January 1862 in the "Three Lime-Trees", an inn formerly situated on the premises.

Until the Second World War, the Prague literati (Egon Erwin Kisch, Max Brod, Ernst Weiß, Ludwig Winder and many others) frequented the **"Café Continental"** [Na Příkopě 17]. The **Sylva-Taroucca Palace** [Na Příkopě 10] is late Baroque and attributed to Kilian Ignaz Dientzenhofer. The sculptural adornments are by Ignaz Franz Platzer. The beautiful staircase is well worth seeing.

Jungmann Square   96
[Jungmannovo nám.] Ⓜ A, B MŮSTEK

This square is named after Josef Jungmann (1773–1847), the founder of the modern Czech written language whose statue was erected here in 1878.

Church of St Mary   97
of the Snows
[Kostel Panny Marie Sněžné, Jungmannovo náměstí] Ⓜ A, B MŮSTEK

In 1347, after his coronation as king of Bohemia, Charles IV founded the Cathedral of "St Mary of the Snows". It was to be the landmark of the newly founded New Town and would have surpassed even St Vitus' Cathedral in size. The choir was completed in 1397, but building work was abandoned at the outbreak of the Hussite wars. The radical Jan Želivský preached here after 1419, when the church had been taken over by the Hussites. In the same year, he led a demonstration from here to the New Town City Hall, eventually culminating in the so-called "First Defenestration of Prague". The tower was destroyed in the Hussite turmoil of 1434; the vault of the Gothic choir collapsed in the 16th century, as a result, it was rebuilt in 1601. The 35 metre high choir towered above all other buildings in the New Town until well into the 19th century. In the 20th century, however, Prague's tallest church became increasingly lost amidst the new commercial

New Town

163

towers and palaces. The church's original impact can now only be rightly estimated from the Franciscan garden or from higher vantage points.

The interior of St Mary of the Snows is still predominantly Gothic; it contains a magnificent Baroque high altar with carvings and sculptures, which is well worth seeing. It is the largest of its kind in Prague. Wenzel Lorenz Reiner painted an altar piece (*The Annunciation*) for the northern side altar.

The former **Franciscan monastery** [Jungmannovo náměstí 18] was once home to the Carmelite order, the Franciscans having settled here around 1600. What once was the monastery cellar is nowadays a wine bar. On the cemetery gates facing Wenceslas Square are portraits of the founders of the monastery, King John of Luxemburg and his son Emperor Charles IV.

The inn **"U Pinkasů"** [Jungmannovo náměstí 16] is situated in a Gothic townhouse with a Renaissance doorway. The Pilsner beer pub was established in 1843 by Jakub Pinkas, the former master tailor to the Franciscans.

The author Anna Lauermann-Miksch (1852–1932), who published under the pseudonym Felix Téver, held well-known literary salons at the **"Salon Lauermann"** [Jungmannovo náměstí 20], a dainty Empire-style building.

magika", a combination of theatre, music, pantomime, film and slide projections was originally housed here; its creator, the director Alfred Radok, introduced his invention at the 1958 World Exhibition in Brussels. During the "Velvet Revolution" of 1989, the opposition "Citizens Forum" held its debates and assemblies here.

During his visit to Prague, Bill Clinton played the saxophone in the **jazz club "Reduta"** [Národní třída 20] – nameplates on the seats commemorate the session. On the first floor of the building is the **"Café Louvre"**, also frequented by Franz Kafka.

The GDR Centre for Culture and Information was based at the **Dunaj Insurance Palace** [Národní třída 10], a 1920s Constructivist palace. The Prague author Gustav Meyrink lived in its predecessor, the Wallis Palace. Bedřich Smetana lived in the **Lažanský Palace** [Národní třída 1] from 1868–1869. Here he wrote his opera The Bartered Bride. The **"Café Slavia"**, popular among artists and writers, has been established here since 1881.

National Street   98

[Národní třída]   Ⓜ B Národní třída

The Adria Palace [Národní třída 40] was built in 1925 for the insurance firm Riunione Adriatica. The world-famous "Laterna

National Theatre   99

[Národní divadlo, Národní třída 2]
Ⓣ 6, 9, 17, 18, 21, 22 Národní divadlo

The grand opening of this theatre and opera house was celebrated on 11th June 1881 with a performance of Smetana's opera *Libuše*; however, only two months after the ceremony, a fire destroyed the building. Nonetheless, the nation was not to be discouraged: donations for the theatre were collected once again and, on April 14th 1883, the strains of *Libuše* resounded anew before the festival audience; this time, the building was to last.

The National Theatre, with a capacity of more than 1,800, is built entirely from regional materials; it is one of the most magnificent neo-Renaissance edifices in Prague. The most prominent contemporary artists contributed to its interior – such as the architect Josef Zítek, the painters Josef Mánes, Mikoláš Aleš, Vojtěch Hynais and Václav Brožík, as well as the sculptors Bohuslav Schnirch and Josef Václav Myslbek. Since then, they have been known to Czech art history as the "Generation of the National Theatre".

The aforementioned "Laterna magika" has found a new home in the **Nová Scéna** (New Scene), the 1970s annexe to the National Theatre: a cube of Cuban marble slabs clad with glass bricks.

St Adalbert's Church 100
[Chrám sv. Vojtěcha, Vojtěšská]
Ⓣ 6, 9, 17, 18, 21, 22 Národní Divadlo

Not far from the National Theatre, close to the embankment, is the somewhat neglected Gothic Church of St Adalbert, in which ceiling frescoes from the first half of the 16th century were discovered. The adjacent Cross Chapel was added in 1690. Antonín Dvořák played the church organ here between 1873 and 1876.

New Town

The National Theatre on the Vltava.

Opposite the church is the rectory, decorated with sculptures by Ignaz Franz Platzer; a memorial has been erected here in honour of the composer Josef Bohuslav Foerster (1859–1951), a friend of Gustav Mahler.

New Town Hall `101`

[Novoměstská radnice, Karlovo náměstí] Ⓜ B KARLOVO NÁMĚSTÍ

The Gothic New Town Hall stands on the large Charles Square, laid out by Charles IV and formerly known as the Cattle Market. The so-called First De-fenestration of Prague took place here on the 30th July 1419.

That day, a furious crowd of followers of the reformer Jan Hus demanded the release of their fellow believers. It is said they were met with derision. In consequence, several Catholic councillors were thrust out of the window and a total of eleven people lost their lives. The event is said to have outraged King Wenceslas to such a degree that the monarch died of a stroke a few days later.

Church of SS Cyril and Methodius `102`

[Kostel sv. Cyrila a Metoděje, Resslova] Ⓜ B KARLOVO NÁMĚSTÍ

The church – formerly St Charles Borromeus' – probably owes its Baroque verve to Kilian Ignaz Dientzenhofer. The Czech paratroopers who assassinated Deputy Reich Protector Reinhard Heydrich on the 27th May 1942 died here on the 18th June 1942. The pursuers had been treacherously tipped-off that the assassins were hiding in the crypt.

There are a small museum and a memorial wall plaque to commemorate these events.

Dancing House `103`

[Tančící dům, Rašínovo nábřeží 80] Ⓜ B KARLOVO NÁMĚSTÍ

This futuristic building by the American architect Frank O. Gehry was erected in the mid-

The New Town City Hall.

The "Dancing House".

Emmaus Monastery 104

[Emauzský klášter, Vyšehrad-
ská 49] Ⓜ B KARLOVO NÁMĚSTÍ

The Benedictine monastery
founded by Charles IV as a
haven for the Slavic liturgy (Na
Slovanech) fell into disrepair in
the Hussite era. This monastery
was consecrated on Easter Mon-
day 1372, thus its name is a
reminder of the Easter gospel,
which tells of the journey of the
disciples to Emmaus. The minster's Baroque spires of were destroyed in February 1945 in an
American bombing raid. The
cycle of frescoes in the monastery cloister created by the court
painters of Charles IV was severely damaged in fighting the fire.

Church at Karlov 105

[Karlov, Ke Karlovu 1]
Ⓜ C I. P. PAVLOVA

Emperor Charles IV had this
high Gothic structure erected in
1350 to commemorate his coronation in Aachen and granted
it to the canons of the Augustine
order, who were summoned from
France. In 1377, after over two
decades of construction works,
the church was dedicated to
Charles the Great and the Assumption of Mary. The Hussites
destroyed the church in 1420;
more than 70 years later, however, the church was reconse-
crated and returned to its original purpose. In the 17th century,
Karlov ("Charles' court") developed into a Baroque place of pilgrimage.

90s on an empty plot that had
been lying waste for decades, a
Second World War bombsite
that had never been rebuilt. The
building's two cylindrical struc-
tures, jokingly known as Fred
Astaire and Ginger Rogers, are
in stark contrast with the surrounding architecture, which is
almost exclusively turn-of-the-
century. In professional circles,
the building is thought to be an
example of "Deconstructivist dis-
aster architecture". The Dancing
House is an office building, only
the ground floor and the restaurant on the roof terrace are open
to the public.

New Town

In the Outskirts

[Na předměstí]

In the Outskirts

Vyšehrad 106

[Vyšehrad] Ⓜ C Vyšehrad

The Vyšehrad citadel, a quiet and mysterious Baroque fortress, lies on a rocky ledge high above the right bank of the Vltava. It is thought that there was an old Slavic castle here, to the south of Prague, in the eighth century; it is not mentioned in writing, however, until the chronicles of the year 1002. Over the centuries, Vyšehrad has been a royal seat, a small market town, Bohemia's religious centre (Vyšehrad's provost was second in the ecclesiastical order of precedence, after the archbishop), a Baroque fortress, and a destination for excursions for the residents of the capital. There is a series of buildings and monuments as a reminder of the hill's eventful history.

St Martin's Rotunda.

"Libuše's Bath"

The **St Martin's Rotunda**, built in the 11th century, is the oldest of its kind to have survived in Prague.

The remnants of rocks and walls rising steeply over the River Vltava are known as **"Libuše's Bath"**. From here the prophetess Libuše is said to have lowered herself down to the river to bathe.

The **Leopold Gate** is a reminder that Vyšehrad was once a mighty military stronghold.

The **Old Deanery** [Soběslavova 1] was the residence of the Dean of the Chapter. It was seriously damaged in a gunpowder explosion of 1760.

The **New Deanery** [Štulcova 4] was built by Provost Václav Štulc in the neo-Gothic style between 1872 and 1874.

The history of the **capitular and parish church of SS Peter and Paul**

On the Vyšehrad

1 Tábor Gate
2 Leopold Gate
3 St Martin's Rotunda
4 Vyšehrad Gate
5 St Wenceslas monument

6 New Deanery
7 Old Deanery
8 Wine tavern "At Vyšehrad"
9 Church of SS Peter and Paul
10 Vyšehrad Cemetery
11 Slavín
12 Libuše's Bath

(cf. pp. 168/169) stretches right back to medieval times. The façade was reconstructed in the 20th century and a neo-Gothic entrance (with a relief of the Last Judgement) was added. Inside the church is a replica of the so-called "Rain Madonna" of Vyšehrad.

The Vyšehrad cemetery includes the **Slavín** monument. This is the last resting place of many eminent personalities of Czech cultural life; among them are Jan Neruda, Alfons Mucha, Bedřich Smetana, Antonín Dvořák, Karel Hynek Mácha, Božena Němcova, Mikoláš Aleš.

Villa Bertramka 107

[Mozartova 2] Ⓣ 4, 7, 9, 10 BERTRAMKA

Villa Bertramka is a small former vineyard in Smíchov, a suburb outside the old city walls. Mozart stayed with his Prague friends František and Josepha Dušek in this idyllic country house in 1787. His opera *Don Giovanni*, which premiered in the Estates' Theatre, is believed to have been completed in the Villa Bertramka.

Outskirts

171

The Mozart-Villa "Bertramka".

The villa is a museum now and, without doubt, the most important memorial to Mozart in Prague. There are seven exhibition rooms in which the stages of Mozart's visits to Prague can be followed; in one room there is a grand piano which Mozart is said to have played. In the estate garden is a statue of 1876 by Thomas Seidan commemorating the composer.

"Belvedere" Heights `108`

[Letná]   Ⓣ 18, 20 CHOTKOVY SADY

As the name suggests, there is a beautiful view from this plateau over the River Vltava and it is a charming destination, especially in summer. There are several eyecatching sights to be seen on a stroll through the park: the **Prime Minister's residence** (Kramář Villa), the peculiar **Hanau**

Hanau Pavilion on Letná Hill.

Pavilion (cast in the ironworks of Prince Wilhelm von Hanau on the occasion of the National Jubilee Exhibition in 1891), or the oversized **metronome** on the concrete plinth that was formerly "adorned" with the world's largest statue of Stalin; erected in the 1950s, when the dictator's time ran out, the monumental group statue was also promptly blown up.

Every year on the 1st May, the Communist government held parades and displays of power on the large **Letná plateau**. In 1989, hundreds of thousands of Czechs came here to protest against the regime.

Žižka Monument 109

[Národní památník Jana Žižky na Vítkově] Ⓜ B, C Florenc, then change to Ⓑ 133, 207 U Památníku

A mighty equestrian figure in front of a granite-clad cube on Vítkov Hill can be seen from afar. Besides the main hall and the Presidents' burial vault, the cube, which was erected between 1927 and 1932 as a national memorial, also contains the Tomb of the Unknown Soldier. The 9 m high equestrian statue was added to the ensemble in 1950 and is a monument to the Hussite Commander Jan Žižka of Trocnov, who triumphed over the Catholic Emperor Sigismund in 1420. The statue, based on a model by Bohumil Kafka, is the largest equestrian statue cast in bronze in the world.

Chateau Troja 110

[Zámek Troja, U Trojského zámku 1] Ⓜ C Nádraží Holešovice, then change to Ⓑ 112 Zoologická zahrada

The Troja Summer Residence, both one of the most magnificent palaces in the country and the masterpiece of Bohemian Baroque, was built for Count Wenzel Adalbert von Sternberg in the years 1680–1688. Architect Jean Baptiste Mathey based the three-winged complex on the French model, while also making good use of first-hand knowledge he had acquired during his years in Rome.

Chateau Troja has a uniquely beautiful open stairway with figures from Greek mythology, which take the triumph of the Olympic gods over the Giants (Gigantomachy) as their theme. The splendidly painted **banquet hall** (Imperial Hall) contains ancestral portraits of the then reigning Habsburg family, scenes from Austrian history (for example, *Victory of the Austrians over the Turks*), as well as representations of heraldic and allegorical subjects, and forms the

Chateau Troja.

central core of the late Baroque chateau complex.

The Municipal Gallery of Prague also has an exhibition of 19th century Czech art within the castle. Chateau Troja was built on the site of an old wine-growing estate, and wine is grown in the area to this day. Lovers of nature can visit not only the Pomological Institute (institute for fruit-growing) in Troja, but also Prague Zoo and the Arboretum [Stromovka], one of the most attractive gardens in Central Europe.

Star Summer Palace   111

[Letohrádek Hvězda, obora Hvězda]   Ⓣ 15, 22, 25   Vypich

In 1530 Emperor Ferdinand I had a game enclosure, surrounded by a protective wall, laid out on the outskirts of the city. In 1555, his son Archduke Ferdinand of Tyrol had the Star (Czech: Hvězda) Summer Palace built in the Renaissance style. He chose to give it the shape of a six-pointed star: Diamond-shaped rooms are found within five of the points, while the sixth houses the staircase – a Renaissance palace without compare in Europe. On the ground floor there is stucco work by Paolo della Stella. The second floor was used for living rooms; the third floor consists of a single 12-sided hall, adorned with frescos and a vaulted, relief-decorated ceiling. The Battle of White Mountain, where the Protestant Bohemian estates were defeated by the Catholic league, was fought on the surrounding grounds.

The Star Summer Palace is a venue for temporary exhibitions of Czech art and culture.

The "Star" Summer Palace.

Gateway to the church
of Our Lady of Victory.

to have carried the miraculous painting of *Mary of Victory* at the head of the victorious army. Wenzel Lorenz Reiner is among the painters of the frescos in the church. A small cairn, not far from the church, marks the exact scene of the battle.

The Church of Our Lady of Victory at White Mountain   **112**

[Kostel Panny Marie Vítězné
na Bílé hoře, Karlovarská 3/6]
Ⓣ 22, 25 Bílá hora

This pilgrimage church stands on the site where, on the 8th November 1620, the army of the Bohemian estates suffered a crushing defeat against the Imperial troops led by Maximilian of Bavaria. Just two years after the battle, a chapel was erected here. The shrine of St Mary is set in the middle of the cloister, bordered with chapels full of paintings and depictions of the miracles wrought by the Holy Virgin. An old Carmelite father is said

Břevnov Monastery   **113**

[Klášter sv. Markéty
v Břevnově, Bělohorská 1]
Ⓣ 15, 22, 25 Břevnovský klášter

This Benedictine abbey is the oldest monastery in Prague and has founded many daughter houses throughout the country. The abbey was established by the second Bishop of Prague, Bishop Adalbert, in 992. The first monks came from Italy and carried relics of Saints Alexius and Boniface with them. The relics of St Margaret, to whom the monastery church is dedicated, were brought to Břevnov later.

The present **minster** was erected in the early 18th century by Christoph Dientzenhofer. Only the crypt remained of the preceding early Romanesque building. The altar pieces in the monastery church are works of Peter Brandl. They depict the *Death of St Benedict* as well as *Death of the Blessed Günther*, a local hermit who was buried on the premises. A ceiling fresco of 1727 in the monastery's **Prelate's Hall** ("Theresian Hall") is also devoted to the death of the devout hermit. It was painted by Cosmas Damian Asam, the master of South German Late Baroque.

Outskirts

Useful Czech Phrases

General

yes	ano
no	ne
please	prosím
thank you	děkuji
excuse me	promiňte
large	velký
small	malý
young	mladý
new	nový
old	starý

Numbers

0	nula
1	jeden, jedna, jedno
2	dva, dvě
3	tři
4	čtyři
5	pět
6	šest
7	sedm
8	osm
9	devět
10	deset
11	jedenáct
12	dvanáct
13	třináct
14	čtrnáct
15	patnáct
16	šestnáct
17	sedmnáct
18	osmnáct
19	devatenáct
20	dvacet
30	třicet
40	čtyřicet
50	padesát
60	šedesát
70	sedmdesát
80	osmdesát
90	devadesát
100	sto
200	dvěstě
1000	tisíc
2000	dva tisíce

Days of the Week

Monday	pondělí
Tuesday	úterý
Wednesday	středa
Thursday	čtvrtek
Friday	pátek
Saturday	sobota
Sunday	neděle

Months

January	leden
February	únor
March	březen
April	duben
May	květen
June	červen
July	červenec
August	srpen
September	září
October	říjen
November	listopad
December	prosinec

Seasons

spring	jaro
summer	léto
autumn	podzim
winter	zima

Getting acquainted

Good morning!	Dobré ráno!
Good day!	Dobrý den!
Good evening!	Dobrý večer!
Good night!	Dobrou noc!
Goodbye!	Na shledanou!
Bye!	Ahoj!
What's your name?	Jak se jmenujete?
My name is ...	Jmenuji se ...
How old are you?	Kolik je Vám let?
I'm ... years old.	Je mi ... let.
Where are you from?	Odkud jste?
I'm from the UK.	Jsem z Velké Británie.
Do you speak English?	Mluvíte anglicky?
How are you?	Jak se máte?
I'm fine.	Mám se dobře.
I speak very little Czech.	Mluvím česky jen trochu.
I don't understand.	Nerozumím.
Could you repeat that please?	Ještě jednou, prosím.

Directions

north	sever

south	jih
east	východ
west	západ
left	nalevo
right	napravo
up	nahoře
down	dole
straight on	rovně
back	zpátky
far	daleko
nearby	blízko
How far is ...?	Jak daleko je ...?
How do I get to ...?	Jak se dostanu ...?
Where is ...?	Kde je ...?

Travelling by train

railway station	nádraží
platform	kolej
train	vlak
ticket	jízdenka
When does the train to Brno leave?	Kdy jede vlak do Brna?
Is this seat still free?	Je to místo volné?
Where is the central station?	Kde je hlavní nádraží?
Is this the price for a return ticket?	Platí tato cena za cestu tam i zpět?

Travelling by car

departure	odjezd
breakdown service	odtahová služba
car	auto
motorway	dálnice
unleaded	natural (bez olova)
diesel	nafta
breakdown	porucha
car park	parkoviště
street	ulice
super	super
fill up	tankovat
petrol station	benzinová pumpa
leaded	olovnatý
garage	autoopravna
How do I get to the motorway to ...?	Jak se dostanu na dálnici na ...?

Food and drink

apple	jablko
apple juice	jablečná šťáva
banana	banán
beef	hovězí maso
beer	pivo
bottle	láhev

bread	chléb
breakfast	snídaně
broccoli	brokolice
butter	máslo
cauliflower	květák
cheese	sýr
cherries	třešně
chicken	kuře
coffee	káva
cucumber	okurek
dessert	moučník
duck	kachna
dumplings	knedlíky
egg	vejce
fish	ryba
fried sausage	klobása
fruit juice	džus
glass	sklenice
goose	husa
grapes	hroznové víno
ham	šunka
ice cream	zmrzlina
jam	marmeláda
lemon	citron
lobster	humr
meat	maso
milk	mléko
mineral water	minerálka
mushrooms	houby
oil	olej
orange juice	pomerančový džus
pear	hruška
pepper	pepř
plums	švestky
pork	vepřové maso
potatoes	brambory
poultry	drůbež
red cabbage	červené zelí
red wine	červené víno
rice	rýže
roast	pečeně
roast pork	vepřová pečeně
roast veal	telecí pečeně
roll	rohlík
rosé wine	rosé
salad	salát
salmon	losos
salt	sůl
sauerkraut	kyselé zelí
sausage	salám
seafood	mořský salát
small sausages	párky
smoked meat	uzené maso
soup	polévka
starters	předkrm
strawberry	jahoda

sugar	cukr
sweets	sladkosti
tea	čaj
trout	pstruh
tuna	tuňák
turkey	krůta
veal	telecí maso
vegetables	zelenina
vinegar	ocet
watermelon	meloun
whipped cream	šlehačka
white cabbage	hlávkové zelí
white coffee	káva s mlékem
white wine	bílé víno
wine	víno

Eating Out

menu	jídelní lístek
dry wine	suché víno
sweet wine	sladké víno
dark beer	černé pivo
lager	světlé pivo
knife	nůž
fork	vidlička
spoon	lžíce
napkin	ubrousek
Where can I find a good restaurant (with Czech cuisine)?	Kde najdu dobrou restauraci (s českou kuchyní)?
The menu, please.	Jídelní lístek, prosím.
What can you recommend?	Můžete mi něco doporučit?
Do you have anything vegetarian?	Máte nějaká vegetariánská jídla?
Is smoking allowed here?	Může se zde kouřit?
I would like ...	Dám si ...
The bill, please.	Účet, prosím.

Accomodation

hotel	hotel
youth hostel	ubytovna (hostel)
double room	dvoulůžkový pokoj
single room	jednolůžkový pokoj
shower	sprcha
toilet	záchod
half board	polopenze
full board	plná penze
reservation	rezervace
I have booked a room.	Rezervoval jsem pokoj.
Do you have any rooms free?	Máte ještě volné pokoje?

Do you have a room for one night?	Máte pokoj na jednu noc?
Are pets allowed?	Je možné vzít s sebou domácí zvířata?

Out and About

bank	banka
bridge	most
castle	hrad
shopping street	nákupní ulice
garden	zahrada
shop	obchod
island	ostrov
church	kostel
museum	muzeum
opera	opera
park	park
square	náměstí
post office	pošta
palace	zámek
telephone box	telefonní budka
theatre	divadlo
bureau de change	směnárna

Pronunciation

á, é, í, ó, ú, ů, ý	are long vowels
c	is pronounced **ts** as in boots
č	pronounced **ch** as in child
ck	pronounced **tsk** (e.g. německy – *nyemetske*)
ě	when following a consonant, pronounced **ye** as in yes.
ř	a particularly difficult sound, pronounced as a combination of **r** and **sh** (as in Dvořák – *Dvorshak*)
r	is rolled
š	**sh** as in shack
ž	as in vision

Essential Information

Unfortunately, contact details like telephone numbers and e-mail addresses are sometimes rather short-lived. Despite all efforts to provide up-to-date information, the publishers can't always guarantee the validity of the details given below.

Accommodation Bureau and Tourist Information

A valuable source of information for visitors to Prague (last-minute reservations, tours, accommodation, special offers, general information etc.) is the multilingual website at www.visitprague.cz .

The accommodation bureau and tourist information centre in the **central station** is open daily from 6 a.m. to 11 p.m.
www.praguehotellocator.com
Ⓜ C HLAVNÍ NÁDRAŽÍ

Prague Information Service (PIS)
[Pražská informační služba]
Staroměstské náměstí 1 • 110 00 Praha 1
Phone: 12 444 • www.pis.cz
Ⓜ A, B MŮSTEK
Tourist information in the Old Town Hall.

Hostels and Guest Houses

For an overview of affordable guest houses and youth hostels in Prague see www.hostelprague.com . Another website of interest for visitors is www.accommodationin czech.com. The page offers on-line bookings and reservations.

Restaurants and Pubs

It is usual to leave about 10% of the bill as a tip in Czech restaurants, provided the service was good. VAT is included in the prices on the menu. A cover charge is not common in Prague, but is asked for in some of the more tourist-oriented restaurants. A very informative website offering exhaustive information on the restaurants and pubs of Prague in both Czech and English is www.czechdineout.com . Learn all there is to know about prices, menus, addresses, telephone numbers, opening hours etc. of most pubs, restaurants, wine bars, cafés, bars, bistros, pizzerias etc. in Prague.

Allegro
Veleslavínova 2a/1098 • 110 00 Praha 1
Phone: 420 221 427 000
www.fourseasons.com/prague
Ⓜ A STAROMĚSTSKÁ
The restaurant in the Four Seasons Hotel has been repeatedly voted the best in the country and in 2007 was the first restaurant in central and eastern Europe to be awarded with a Michelin Star. This is an upmarket establishment.

U Zlaté hrušky
Nový svět 3 • 11 000 Praha 1
Phone: 220 514 778
www.uzlatehrusky.eu
Ⓣ 22 BRUSNICE
Bohemian and international delicacies in the picturesque "New World" – and of course, it wouldn't be the "Golden Pear" without some amazing pear dishes. The restaurant for special occasions.

Novoměstský pivovar
Vodičkova 20 • 110 00 Praha 1
Phone: 222 232 448 • www.npivovar.cz
Ⓣ 3, 9, 14, 24 Vodičkova
Hearty Czech cuisine with a rustic ambience. The small in-house brewery uses exclusively local ingredients.

Olympia
Vítězná 7 • 110 00 Praha 1
Phone: 251 511 080 • www.kolkovna.cz
Ⓣ 6, 9, 12, 20, 22 Újezd
A large inn belonging to the Kolkovna-group: the whole range from Pilsner Urquell to Bohemian Schnitzel for a reasonable price.

U Malířů
Maltézské náměstí 11 • 118 00 Praha 1
Phone: 257 530 318 • www.umaliru.cz
Ⓣ 12, 20, 22 Hellichova
Traditional French cuisine is served on these historic premises on Maltézské náměstí in the Lesser Town – even Rudolph II was a guest at U Malířů, "the Painters".

Pálffy Palác
Valdštejnská 14 • 101 00 Praha 1
Phone: 257 530 522 • www.palffy.cz
Ⓜ A Malostranská
Finest cuisine, courteous staff and the charm of aristocratic refinement: a candle-lit dinner in the Baroque salon of Pálffy Palace in the Lesser Town is a unique experience.

U Modré kachničky
Nebovidská 6 • 110 00 Praha 1
Phone: 257 320 308
www.umodrekachnicky.cz
Ⓣ 12, 20, 22 Hellichova
As well as its specialities of poultry and game, vegetarian dishes are also served at the quaint "Blue Duck".

U Fleků (cf. p. 30)
Křemencova 11 • 110 00 Praha 1
Phone: 224 934 019-20 • www.ufleku.cz
Ⓜ B Národní třída
Legendary inn in the New Town of Prague; established in 1499, spread out over eight beer halls and home to a famous in-house brewery.

Hostinec U Kalicha
Na Bojišti 12–14 • 120 00 Praha 2
Phone: 296 189 600-01 • www.ukalicha.cz
Ⓜ C I. P. Pavlova
"The Fateful Adventures of the Good Soldier Švejk" began at the inn U Kalicha – today an international crowd enjoys the food and drink here.

Fine dining in the Lesser Town: the Restaurant at Pálffy Palace.

Coffee Houses and Cafés

Grand Hotel Evropa
Václavské náměstí 25 • 110 00 Praha 1
Phone: 224 215 387 • www.evropahotel.cz
Ⓜ A, B Můstek
The most beautiful Art Nouveau café in Prague. Occasional live piano music.

Café Kaaba
Mánesova 20 • 120 00 Praha 2
Phone: 222 254 021 • www.kaaba.cz
Ⓜ A Náměstí Míru
Cheerful and colourful café. The retro interior evokes the times of Caterina Valente and creates a 1950s fairyland.

Café Kabinet
Terronská 25 • 160 00 Praha 6
Phone: 233 326 668
Ⓜ A Dejvická
Off the beaten tourist track: good coffee and lovely cakes are served among old globes – and from the ceiling, a wooden fish-skeleton greets the guests below.

Café Louvre (cf. p. 164)
Národní 22 • 110 00 Praha 1
Phone: 224 930 949
www.cafelouvre.cz
Ⓜ B Národní třída
Traditional coffee-house with several pool tables. Kafka and Rilke were among the guests at the "Louvre".

Café Medúza
Belgická 17 • 120 00 Praha 2
Phone: 222 515 107 • www.meduza.cz
Ⓜ A Náměstí Míru
The café of choice for late risers in the Vinohrady district. There are regular art exhibitions in the adjoining room.

Grand Café Orient
Ovocný trh 19 • 110 00 Praha 1
Phone: 224 224 240
www.grandcaforient.cz
Ⓜ B Náměstí Republiky
The only Cubist coffee-house in the world, with marble tables, a parquet floor and large panoramic windows.

Café Savoy
Vítězná 5 • 150 00 Praha 5
Phone: 257 311 562
Ⓣ 6, 9, 12, 20, 22 Újezd
A grand café with a distinguished history, a very beautiful interior and excellent cuisine.

In the Café Louvre.

The Grand Café Orient.

In the Café Slavia.

Kavárna Slavia (cf. p. 164)
Smetanovo nábřeží 2 • 110 00 Praha 1
Phone: 224 218 493 • www.cafeslavia.cz
Ⓣ 6, 9, 17, 18, 21, 22 Národní divadlo
Traditionally the café of choice for visitors to the neighbouring National Theatre. In the first half of the 20th century, this café was frequented by many artists and intellectuals. They were mainly Czechs – hence the name Slavia – but Guillaume Apollinaire and Rainer Maria Rilke also honoured the Slavia with their presence. Even today, this large café still offers a beautiful view of the bustling city through the large panoramic windows.

Kávarna in the Municipal House
[Obecní dům] (cf. p.124)
náměstí Republiky 5 • 111 21 Praha 1
Phone: 222 002 763
Ⓜ B Náměstí Republiky
Elegant café in the Art Nouveau style; tables are set up on the square in front of the café in summer.

The Kávarna in the Municipal House.

Internet-Cafés

Bohemia Bagel
Masná 2 • 110 00 Praha 1
Phone: 224 812 560
www.bohemiabagel.cz
Ⓜ B Náměstí Republiky
Internet and phone connections, coffee and snacks, along with a playroom for children.

Café Anděl
Na Bělidle 27/302 • 150 00 Praha 5
Phone: 257 324 514 • www.cafeandel.wz.cz
Ⓜ B Anděl
Highspeed internet surfing, accompanied by coffee or a cocktail.

Club Net Café
Americká 39 • 120 00 Praha 2
Phone: 602 466 293
Ⓜ A Náměstí Míru
Internet café close to Náměstí míru, offers printing and scanning services.

Káva Káva Káva
Národní 416/37 • 110 00 Praha 1
Phone: 224 228 862 • www.kava-coffee.cz
Ⓜ B Národní třída
Small courtyard-café with internet access that attracts a young crowd.

Spika
Dlážděná 4 • 110 00 Praha 1
Phone: 224 211 521
www.netcafe.spika.cz
Ⓜ B Náměstí Republiky
Internet café with up-to-date equipment. Computers have headphones, printers are provided.

Cultural Events

Besides the regular tourist information, the Prague Information Centre (PIS) offers a list of concerts and events on their webpage www.pis.cz. Printed cultural listings are available at newsstands – a monthly overview of events ranging from the premiere of an opera to the latest highlights of Prague's night life.

Advance Booking

Ticketpro
Klimentská 22 • 110 00 Praha 1
Phone: 234 704 234 • www.ticketpro.cz
Ⓜ B NÁMĚSTÍ REPUBLIKY

Bohemia Ticket
Na Příkopě 16 • 110 00 Praha 1
Phone: 224 215 031
www.bohemiaticket.cz
Ⓜ A, B MŮSTEK

Calendar of Events

January
New Year's concerts: Several venues hold
New Year's concerts on the 1st January. The
Prague Philharmonic Orchestra's concert
at the Rudolfinum is particularly popular.

Prague Winter: The Rudolfinum also
hosts this popular international music and
theatre festival.

February
Holiday World: This large trade fair offers
numerous attractions and is held on the
exhibition grounds of Výstaviště.

March
Matthew-Fair: Prague's oldest funfair
still excites both the young and the young
at heart, with merry-go-rounds and other
attractions on the exhibition grounds of
Výstaviště.

At the fun fair.

The **Festival of Contemporary Music**
offers concerts by the best local musicians
at Obecní dům.

The Lucerna and Aero cinemas contrib-
ute to the **European Film Festival** with
alternative cinema and retrospectives.

April
Mozart Open: This comparatively small
series of concerts stages the composer's
lesser known works in the Villa Bertramka.

The **International Jazz Festival** hosted
by the Lucerna has become one of the
most prominent and prestigious in Europe.

May
Every year, the famous classical music festival **Prague Spring** brings a large number of international artists to Prague, per-
forming in venues across the city from
mid-May to mid-June. Tickets should be
booked well in advance (www.festival.cz).

The **Prague Book Fair** has been held on
the exhibition grounds of Výstaviště since
1995, and many regional and international publishers present their latest publications every year in mid-May.

June
Dance Prague, an amazing and ambitious
contemporary dance show, can be seen at
Divadlo Archa (www.archatheatre.cz).

July
At the **Folklore Festival**, music and dance
groups from all over the country perform
at various venues across town; the main
shows are at Wenceslas Square and Old
Town Square.

August
A summer highlight is the three week
long **Verdi Festival** staged at the State
Opera every August.

September
Music lovers shouldn't miss the **Prague
Autumn** music and theatre festival in the
Rudolfinum.

October
"Burčák" (new wine) from Moravia is served in many Prague restaurants.

November
During the **German-Language Theatre Festival**, both contemporary and classical plays from Germany, Austria and Switzerland are staged at various venues in Prague.

December
Christmas markets are held on the Old Town Square and other squares throughout the city centre, with the usual selection of stands selling mulled wine, sausages and handicrafts etc.

The best view of the **New Year's fireworks** is from Prague Castle. Anyone fond of company (and noise) might choose to watch the spectacle from Charles Bridge along with thousands of others, locals and visitors alike.

The Musical Theatre in Karlín.

Interior of the National Theatre.

Concerts, Operas, Plays

Musical Theatre Karlín
[Hudební divadlo Karlín]
Křižíkova 10 • 186 00 Praha 8
Phone: 221 868 111 • www.hdk.cz
Ⓜ B Křižíkova
Musicals and operettas staged against a grand, faux-Baroque backdrop.

Laterna magika (cf. p. 164, 165)
Národní třída 4 • 110 00 Praha 1
Phone: 224 931 482 • www.laterna.cz
Ⓣ 6, 9, 17, 18, 21, 22 Národní divadlo
Multimedia shows combining elements of pantomime, dance, music, light and projections.

National Theatre (cf. p. 164)
[Národní divadlo]
Národní 2 • 112 30 Praha 1
Phone: 224 901 448
www.narodni-divadlo.cz
Ⓣ 6, 9, 17, 18, 21, 22 Národní divadlo
This magnificent building on the banks of the Vltava offers mainly Czech operas in an authentic atmosphere.

Interior of the State Opera.

Municipal House (cf. p. 126)
[Obecní dům]
náměstí Republiky 5 • 111 21 Praha 1
Phone: 222 002 101 • www.obecnidum.cz
Ⓜ B Náměstí Republiky
Classical concerts are held on a regular basis in the beautiful (Art Nouveau) Smetana Hall.

Rudolfinum (cf. p. 153)
Alšovo nábřeží 12 • 110 01 Praha 1
Phone: 227 059 352 • www.rudolfinum.cz
www.ceskafilharmonie.cz
Ⓜ A Staroměstská
Home to the Czech Philharmonic orchestra, the Rudolfinum also presents soloists and orchestras of international renown.

St. Nicholas' Church in the Old Town
[Chrám sv. Mikuláše] (cf. p. 120)
Staroměstské náměstí 27a
110 01 Praha 1 • Phone: 224 190 994
Ⓜ A Staroměstská
Every day, classical music resounds in this church on the Old Town Square.

Prague State Opera (cf. p. 160)
[Státní opera Praha]
Wilsonova 4 • 110 00 Praha 1
Phone: 224 227 266 • www.opera.cz
Ⓜ A, C Muzeum
The State Opera is Prague's traditional venue for an international operatic repertoire, ranging from Verdi to Wagner.

Estates' Theatre (cf. 129)
[Stavovské divadlo]
Ovocný trh 1 • 110 00 Praha 1
Phone: 224 901 448
www.stavovskedivadlo.cz
www.narodni-divadlo.cz
Ⓜ A, B Můstek
The Estates' Theatre offers first-rate operas and occasionally also plays. Mozart's operas (and especially Don Giovanni) are at the core of the repertoire.

Theatre on the Balustrade
[Divadlo Na zábradlí]
Anenské náměstí 5 • 115 33 Praha 1
Phone: 222 868 868 • www.nazabradli.cz
Ⓣ 17, 18 Karlovy lázně
Close to Charles Bridge and famous for straight theatre, this venue will forever be associated with director Jan Grossmann and playwright Václav Havel.

A glance at the Municipal Library.

Venues in which the City Gallery Prague holds exhibitions
[Galerie hlavního města Prahy]
www.citygalleryprague.cz

Old Town Hall (cf. p. 118)
[Staroměstská radnice]
Staroměstské náměstí 1 • 110 00 Praha 1
Phone: 224 482 751
Opening hours:
Daily 10 a.m.–6 p.m. except Mondays
Ⓜ A, B Můstek
The museum is on the second floor and hosts temporary exhibitions of modern art.

House "At the Golden Ring"
[Dům U Zlatého prstenu]
Týnská 6 • 110 00 Praha 1
Phone: 224 827 022-4
Opening hours:
Daily 10 a.m.–6 p.m. except Mondays
Ⓜ B Náměstí Republiky
20ᵗʰ century Czech art is displayed over three floors.

Bílek Villa [Bílkova vila]
Mickiewiczova 1 • 160 00 Praha 6
Phone: 224 322 021
Opening hours: Daily except Mondays
May–October 10 a.m.–6 p.m.
Ⓣ 18, 20 Chotkovy sady
The works of the sculptor František Bílek are displayed here, in his former home.

Municipal Library [Městská knihovna]
Mariánské náměstí 1 • 110 00 Praha 1
Phone: 222 310 489, 222 313 357
Opening hours:
Daily 10 a.m.–6 p.m. except Mondays
Ⓜ A Staroměstská
The museum is on the second floor. Temporary modern art exhibitions.

House "At the Stone Bell" (cf. p. 121)
[Dům U Kamenného zvonu]
Staroměstské náměstí 13
110 00 Praha 1 • Phone: 224 827 526
Opening hours:
Daily 10 a.m.–6 p.m. except Mondays.
Ⓜ A, B Můstek
Temporary modern art exhibitions.

Chateau Troja (cf. p. 173)
[Trojský zámek]
U Trojského zámku 1 • 170 00 Praha 7
Phone: 283 851 614
Opening hours:
Summer: Daily 10 a.m.–6 p.m. except
Mondays, Winter: Saturdays and Sundays
only 10 a.m.–5 p.m.
Ⓜ C Nádraží Holešovice, then change to
Ⓑ 112 Zoologická zahrada
The museum houses an exhibition of 19ᵗʰ century Czech painting as well as Czech sculpture from 1900–1970.

The Jewish Museum
[Židovské muzeum]

U Staré školy 1 • 110 00 Praha 1
Phone: 221 711 511
www.jewishmuseum.cz

The museum was founded in 1906 and documents the long tradition of Jewish life in Bohemia. All institutions of the Jewish Museum are open daily except Saturdays and Jewish holidays.
Opening hours:
Nov.–Mar. 9 a.m.–4.30 p.m.
Apr.–Oct. 9 a.m.–6 p.m.

Entry costs 300,- Kč and the ticket is also valid for the Old Jewish Cemetery (cf. p. 150) and the following institutions of the Jewish Museum:

Old Ceremonial Hall (cf. p. 150)
[Obřadní síň – budova
pražského Pohřebního bratrstva]
U Starého hřbitova 3a • 110 00 Praha 1
Ⓜ A Staroměstská
An exhibition documenting the work of the Funeral Brethren and giving information about Jewish funeral rites.

Robert Guttmann Gallery
[Galerie Roberta Guttmanna]
U Staré školy 3 • 110 00 Praha 1
Ⓜ A Staroměstská
This gallery of the Jewish Museum was named after Robert Guttmann, a painter of the First Republic, born in the Šumava. Guttmann, who had lived in Prague since 1895, was a strong sympathizer with the Zionist movement, then in its infancy. He died in 1942 in the ghetto of Łódź.

"Klausen" Synagogue (cf. p. 151)
[Klausová synagoga]
U Starého hřbitova 1 • 110 00 Praha 1
Phone: 221 711 511
Ⓜ A Staroměstská
The museum is dedicated to Jewish traditions and rites ranging from religious festivities to everyday customs like kosher cooking.

Maisel Synagogue (cf. p. 147)
[Maiselova synagoga]
Maiselova 8–10 • 110 00 Praha 1
Phone: 221 711 511
Ⓜ A Staroměstská
Part of the collection of "Silver from Bohemian Synagogues" is on display along with an exhibition on the history of Jews in Bohemia

Pinkas' Synagogue (cf. p. 151)
[Pinkasova synagoga]
Široká 3 • 110 00 Praha 1
Phone: 222 326 660
Ⓜ A Staroměstská
Inside the synagogue is a memorial to the victims of the holocaust. There is also an exhibition of paintings by children from the Theresienstadt [Terezín] concentration camp.

Spanish Synagogue (cf. p. 152)
[Španělská synagoga]
Dušní 12/Vězeňská 1 • 110 01 Praha 1
Phone: 224 819 464
Ⓜ A Staroměstská
An exhibition charts the history of Jews in Bohemia from the Jewish emancipation in the 19ᵗʰ century to the present.

Exhibition Venues belonging to Prague Municipal Museum

[Muzeum hlavního města Prahy]
www.muzeumprahy.cz

Main Building [Hlavní budova]
Na Poříčí 52 • 180 00 Praha 8
Phone: 224 816 773
Opening hours:
Daily 9 a.m.–6 p.m. except Mondays.
Ⓜ B, C FLORENC
The museum follows the development of Prague from primeval times to the year 1784. The star attraction is the paper cityscape by Antonín Langweil: covering 20 m², it faithfully reproduces some 2000 Prague buildings as they appeared in the 19ᵗʰ century.

Villa Müller (also Villa Loos) (cf. p. 29)
[Müllerova vila (Loosova vila)]
Nad Hradním vodojemem 14
162 00 Praha 6 • Phone: 224 312 012
vila.muller@volny.cz
Opening hours:
April–October: Tues., Thurs., Sat.
and Sun. 9 a.m.–6 p.m.
November–March Tues., Thurs., Sat.
and Sun. 10 a.m.–5 p.m.
Ⓣ 1, 2, 18 OŘECHOVKA
This villa by the Austrian architect Adolf Loos can only be visited by prior reservation

via the telephone number or e-mail address indicated above.

Výtoň
Rašínovo nábřeží 412 • 120 00 Praha 2
Phone: 224 919 833
Opening hours:
Daily 10 a.m.–6 p.m. except Mondays
Ⓣ 3, 7, 16, 17, 21 VYTON
This museum, housed in the former customs office, charts the history of timber rafting and steam navigation on the Vltava.

Exhibition Venues belonging to the National Museum

[Národní muzeum]
www.nm.cz

National Museum (Main Building)
[Národní muzeum] (cf. p. 158)
Václavské náměstí 68 • 115 79 Praha 1
Phone: 224 497 111
Opening hours:
May–September 10 a.m.–6 p.m.
October–April 9 a.m.–5 p.m.
Ⓜ A, C MUZEUM
This majestic building dominates the upper end of Wenceslas Square, housing extensive scientific and archaeological collections. The museum was established in 1818 and is both the largest and the oldest Czech museum.

Langweil's model in the Prague City Museum (Scale 1:480).

The "Villa Amerika" (Dvořák Museum).

Antonín Dvořák Museum (cf. p. 37)
[Muzeum Antonína Dvořáka]
Ke Karlovu 20 • 120 00 Praha 2
Phone: 224 923 363
Opening hours:
Daily 10 a.m.–5 p.m. except Mondays
Ⓜ C I.P. Pavlova
The museum in the Baroque "Vila Amerika" houses the famous Czech composer Antonín Dvořák's study and several of his manuscript scores.

Bedřich Smetana Museum (cf. p. 135)
[Muzeum Bedřicha Smetany]
Novotného lávka 1 • 110 00 Praha 1
Phone: 222 220 082
Opening hours:
Daily 10 a.m.–12 a.m. and 12.30–5 p.m. except Tuesdays
Ⓣ 17, 18 Karlovy lázně
Besides the composer's original manuscripts and letters, the museum also exhibits Smetana's piano and many costumes from his operas.

Lapidarium [Lapidárium]
Výstaviště 422 • 170 00 Praha 7
Phone: 233 375 636
Opening hours:
Tuesday–Friday 12 a.m.–6 p.m. and Saturday/Sunday 10 a.m.–6 p.m.
Ⓣ 5, 12, 17 Výstaviště
This building of 1891 houses sculptures from all stylistic periods, including originals from Charles Bridge.

Palace Lobkowicz (cf. p. 86)
[Lobkovický palác] • Jiřská 3
119 08 Praha 1 • Phone: 233 354 467
Opening hours:
Daily 10.30 a.m.–6 p.m. except Mondays
Ⓜ A Malostranská
This spacious palace houses an exhibition on national history.

The Czech Museum of Music
[České muzeum hudby] (cf. p. 37)
Karmelitská 2/4 • 118 00 Praha 1
Phone: 257 257 777
Opening hours:
Daily 10 a.m.–6 p.m. except Tuesdays
Ⓣ 12, 20, 22 Hellichova
This modern museum has found a home in a former Baroque church and displays a large variety of musical instruments and related items. Occasionally, concerts are also held here.

The Lapidarium.

Ethnological Museum
[Náprstkovo muzeum]
Betlémské náměstí 1 • 110 00 Praha 1
Phone: 224 497 501 • www.aconet.cz/npm
Opening hours:
Daily 10 a.m.–6 p.m. except Mondays
Ⓜ B Národní třída
Several permanent exhibitions offer interesting insights into the cultures of indigenous people in America, Asia, Australia and Oceania.

Exhibition Venues belonging to the National Gallery

[Národní galerie]
www.ngprague.cz

Palace Kinsky [Palác Kinských] (cf. p. 120)
Staroměstské náměstí 12
110 15 Praha 1 • Phone: 224 810 758
Opening hours:
Daily 10 a.m.–6 p.m. except Mondays
Ⓜ A, B Můstek
The palace houses the permanent exhibition "The Landscape in Czech Art (17th–20th Centuries)".

Convent of St Agnes of Bohemia

[Klášter sv. Anežky České] (cf. p. 141)
U Milosrdných 17/Anežská 1
110 00 Praha 1 • Phone: 224 810 628
Opening hours:
Daily 10 a.m.–6 p.m. except Mondays
Ⓜ A Staroměstská
A collection of medieval art and crafts is exhibited in this former convent.

Trade Fair Palace – Collection of Modern and Contemporary Art

[Veletržní palác – Sbírka moderního a současného umění]
Dukelských hrdinů 47
170 00 Praha 7 • Phone: 224 301 111
Opening hours:
Daily 10 a.m.–6 p.m. except Mondays
Ⓣ 5, 12, 17 Veletržní
Works by international artists from the 19th to 20th centuries are exhibited over several floors of this Functionalistic building. Tickets are available for individual floors.

Museum of Czech Cubism (House of the Black Madonna)

[Muzeum českého kubismu (Dům U Černé Matky Boží)]
Ovocný trh 19 • 110 00 Praha 1
Phone: 224 211 746
Opening hours:
Daily 10 a.m.–6 p.m. except Mondays
Ⓜ A, B Můstek
The first Cubist residential house in Europe is now home to a noteworthy collection of objects of Czech Cubism.

St George's Convent

[Klášter sv. Jiří]
Jiřské náměstí 33 • 119 00 Praha 1
Phone: 257 531 644
Opening hours:
Daily 10 a.m.–6 p.m. except Mondays
Ⓣ 22 Pražský hrad
A collection of Mannerist and Baroque art from Bohemia (works by Karel Škréta, Peter Brandl, Adrian de Vries, for example).

Chateau Zbraslav

[Zámek Zbraslav]
Bartoňova 2 • 156 00 Praha 5
Phone: 257 921 638-39
Opening hours:
Daily 10 a.m.–6 p.m. except Mondays
Ⓜ B Smíchovské nádraží, then change to
Ⓑ 129, 241, 243, 314, 318, 338, 390 Zbraslavské náměstí
The castle is now used as a museum for Asian art. Beside Chinese and Japanese art, there are Indian and Tibetan pieces as well as exhibits from the Near East.

Exhibits in the Museum of Czech Cubism.

Schwarzenberg Palace (cf. p. 68)
[Schwarzenberský palác]
Hradčanské náměstí 15 • 118 00 Praha 1
Phone: 233 081 713
Opening hours:
Daily 10 a.m.–6 p.m. except Mondays
Ⓣ 22 PRAŽSKÝ HRAD
The sgraffittoed palace houses a permanent exhibition on "Baroque in Bohemia".

Sternberg Palace (cf. p. 67)
[Šternberský palác]
Hradčanské náměstí 15 • 118 00 Praha 1
Phone: 233 090 570
Opening hours:
Daily 10 a.m.–6 p.m. except Mondays
Ⓣ 22 PRAŽSKÝ HRAD
An extensive collection of European art from classical antiquity to the Baroque era; besides noted Dutch masters there are also works by Tiepolo, El Greco, Goya, Dürer, Holbein and Lukas Cranach.

Other Museums

Bertramka (cf. p. 37, 171)
Mozartova 169 • 150 00 Praha 5
Phone: 257 317 465
www.bertramka.com
Opening hours:
April–October 9.30 a.m.–6 p.m.
November–March 9.30 a.m.–4 p.m.
Ⓣ 4, 7, 9, 10 BERTRAMKA
The most important memorial to Mozart in Prague. Concerts are held in summer, sometimes in the villa's picturesque garden.

Interior of Villa Bertramka.

Arts-and-Crafts Museum (cf. p. 153)
[Uměleckoprůmyslové muzeum]
17. listopadu 2 • 110 00 Praha 1
Phone: 251 093 111 • www.upm.cz
Opening hours:
Daily except Mondays 10 a.m.–6 p.m.,
Tuesdays 10 a.m.–7 p.m.
Ⓜ A STAROMĚSTSKÁ
The largest collection of glass in the world, displaying a total of more than 16,000 exhibits of glass and chinaware as well as pottery. In addition, there is a section dedicated to clocks, measuring instruments and Cubist furniture.

Franz Kafka Museum
[Muzeum Franze Kafky]
Cihelná 2b • 110 00 Praha 1
Phone: 221 451 400
www.kafkamuseum.cz
Opening hours: Daily 10 a.m.–6 p.m.,
January/February 11 a.m.–5 p.m.
Ⓜ A MALOSTRANSKÁ
Informative exhibition on the life and works of the famous Prague writer.

Kampa Museum (Sova Mills) (cf. p. 103)
[Museum Kampa (Sovovy mlýnů)]
U Sovových mlýnu 2 • 118 00 Praha 1
Phone: 257 286 147
www.museumkampa.cz
Opening hours: Daily 10 a.m.–6 p.m.
Ⓣ 6, 9, 12, 20, 22 ÚJEZD
The museum houses works by 20ᵗʰ century Czech artists.

Prague Loretto Shrine [Loreta] (cf. p. 63)
Loretánské nám. 7 • 118 00 Praha 1
Phone: 220 516 740 • www.loreta.cz
Opening hours: Daily except Mondays 9
a.m.–12.15 p.m. and 1 p.m.–4.30 p.m.
Ⓣ 22 POHOŘELEC
The museum of this Marian pilgrimage site houses the Loretto Treasure, a collection of sacred objets d'art from the 16ᵗʰ–18ᵗʰ centuries. The most precious item is a monstrance studded with 6,222 diamonds.

Alfons Mucha Museum
[Muzeum Alfonse Muchy]
Panská 7 • 110 00 Praha 1
Phone: 224 216 415 • www.mucha.cz
Opening hours: Daily 10 a.m.–6 p.m.
Ⓜ A, B MŮSTEK
Around 100 exhibits give a profound insight into the work of the versatile Art Nouveau artist Alfons Mucha (1860–1939).

Alfons Mucha: The Feather.

Prague Castle Gallery

[Obrazárna Pražského hradu]
Prague Castle – Second Courtyard
119 08 Praha 1 • Phone: 224 373 531
www.obrazarna-hradu.cz
Opening hours: Daily 9 a.m.–6 p.m.
(9 a.m.–4 p.m. in winter)
Ⓣ 22 PRAŽSKÝ HRAD
The museum is home to the remainder of the legendary collections of Rudolph II as well as works by Tintoretto, Titian and Rubens.

Police Museum   [Muzeum Policie ČR]

Ke Karlovu 1 • 120 00 Praha 2
Phone: 224 923 619
Opening hours:
Daily 10 a.m.–5 p.m. except Mondays
Ⓜ C I.P. PAVLOVA
This museum boasts a display of police weaponry and a reconstructed crime scene alongside reports of famous criminal cases; it also provides some interesting information about the history of the Czech police force.

Toy Museum   [Muzeum hraček]

Jiřská 6 • 119 01 Praha 1
Phone: 224 372 294
Opening hours: Daily 9.30 a.m.–5.30 p.m.
Ⓣ 22 PRAŽSKÝ HRAD
This museum houses the second largest toy collection in the world. The exhibits cover the whole range from antiquity to the present day.

Strahov Picture Gallery   (cf. p. 57)

[Strahovská obrazárna]
Strahovské nádvoří 1 • 118 00 Praha 1
Phone: 233 107 722
www.strahovskyklaster.cz
Opening hours:
Daily 9 a.m.–12 a.m. and 12.30–5 p.m.
Ⓣ 22 POHOŘELEC
The monastery's important collection includes Gothic paintings – such as the famous Strahov Madonna, works of the Baroque and Rococo eras and a selection of 19th century art.

Tramway Museum

[Muzeum městské hromadné dopravy]
Patočkova 4 • 162 00 Praha 6
Phone: 296 124 900-5
www.dpp.cz/muzeum-mhd
Opening hours:
April–November Saturdays, Sundays, public holidays 9 a.m.–5 p.m.
Ⓣ 1, 2, 18 VOZOVNA STŘEŠOVICE
More than 40 vintage streetcars are on display in this museum, established in the Střešovice depot since 1993, as are many other exhibits illustrating the history of public transport in Prague

The Tramway Museum.

191

National Museum of Technology
[Národní technické muzeum]
Kostelní 42 • 170 78 Praha 7
Phone: 220 399 111 • www.ntm.cz
Opening hours:
Daily 9 a.m.–5 p.m. except Mondays.
Ⓣ 1, 8, 15, 25, 26 LETENSKÉ NÁMĚSTÍ
Machinery of all kinds from the beginnings of the Industrial Revolution to the present day is spread out across the 6,000 m² of the Museum of Technology. Established in 1941, it offers more than just cars, aeroplanes and other vehicles: underneath the building, you can visit a model of a coal mine, nearly a kilometre in length. In addition, educational trails on the subject of optical and acoustic perception have been installed.

Wax Museum Prague
[Muzeum voskových figurín]
Melantrichova 5 • 112 79 Praha 1
Phone: 224 229 852
www.waxmuseumprague.cz
Opening hours:
Daily 9 a.m.–8 p.m.
Ⓜ A, B MŮSTEK
This display of waxworks brings you face to face with both Czech and international personalities of the 20th and 21st centuries. There is also a "Grandstand of the Dictators of the World".

Cinema and Film

Czech cinematography has a very good reputation; many Czech productions (*Kolja* for example) have been able to hold their own on the international market. Any film buff must have heard of the Czech-American director Miloš Forman (*Amadeus*). Several major films have recently been shot in the lanes of Prague, and surely no history of film would be complete without mentioning the Barrandov Film Studios.
Not knowing Czech is no bar to seeing a movie in Prague. Most international films are shown in their original languages with Czech subtitles. There are a couple of Czech websites that provide information on current movies and the latest news from the world of cinema:

www.novinky.cz/kultura/prehled
www.kinoserver.cz

Newspapers and the Media

A wide selection of daily and weekly international newspapers and magazines can be found at newsstands in the city centre or in larger hotels. The German *Prager Zeitung* (www.pragerzeitung.cz) and the English *Prague Post* (www.praguepost.cz) are weekly local newspapers and both offer a large section on current events. Radio Praha's international programmes are highly interesting and it is also well worth having a look at the station's informative website: www.radio.cz.

Weather and Climate

Prague has a continental climate. In summer it can get rather hot, as the city nestles in a basin between the hills. The most pleasant temperatures are from May to June and from September to October. Winters are relatively mild, although there can be occasional sharp frosts. Anyone wishing to avoid the overcrowded summer months would be charmed by wintry, snowy Prague, especially as winter is the high season for concerts and operas.

Czech Public Holidays

01.01.	New Year
variable:	Easter Monday
01.05.	Labour Day
08.05.	Liberation Day (from NS Occupation)
05.07.	Saints Cyril and Methodius' Day
06.07.	Jan Hus' Day
28.09.	St Wenceslas' Day (Czech Statehood Day)
28.10.	Foundation of the Czechoslovak Republic
17.11.	Day of the Struggle for Freedom and Democracy
24.12.	Christmas Eve
25.12.	Christmas Day
26.12.	Second Christmas Holiday (St Stephen)

Prague by Taxi

AAA Taxi	222 333 222
Halotaxi	244 114 411
ProfiTaxi	261 314 151

Taxis are quite cheap in Prague, but there are some black sheep among the drivers who will demand exaggerated fares from unsuspecting tourists. Thus it is advisable to ask the fare before setting off. As a rule, taxis belonging to hotels and at the airport are slightly more expensive. Calling a taxi from the companies above will considerably reduce the danger of being cheated. The operator may speak English and occasionally other languages too.

Bus, Tram and Metro

The public transport network in Prague is very efficient. Tickets

Down to the Prague Metro.

for buses, the metro and trams can be bought from ticket offices and vending machines within the metro stations or some tobacconists [trafika]. The tickets have to be validated before entering the platform. All three metro lines operate from 5 a.m. to midnight every three to five minutes; buses and trams [tramvaj] run between 4.30 a.m. and midnight, with some lines operating round the clock. In the daytime buses and trams run every 10 minutes, while at night the interval often increases to 40 minutes. On trams, the name of the next stop is announced shortly before arrival – but so is the name of the stop after that [„příští zastávka"], so be careful not to get off too soon!

Metro and tram maps are available at larger metro stations (such as Muzeum, Můstek or Anděl). You can also look up Prague's streets and lanes online at www.amapy.cz. The site offers a detailed map and information on hotels, museums and restaurants in the vicinity.

Tickets and Fares

Ticket for a 20 minute bus ride
(without changing bus) or
5 stops by metro or tram
including changes for a
maximum of 30 minutes   18,- Kč
    Child fare   9,- Kč
Ticket for a 75 minute ride
on working days (90 minutes
on weekends and public
holidays) including changes   26,- Kč
    Child fare   13,- Kč
Day ticket   100,- Kč
    [Denní jízdenka]
    Child fare   50,- Kč
3-day ticket   330,- Kč
    [Třídenní jízdenka]
5-day ticket   500,- Kč
    [Pětidenní jízdenka]
Monthly ticket   550,- Kč
    [Měsíční jízdenka]

Up-to-date information can be found on-
line at www.dpp.cz

To the Aiport

Prague-Ruzyně airport is situated
20 km northwest of the city
centre and is served by numerous international airlines. It takes
about 30 to 50 minutes from the
airport into the city, however
you travel.
A taxi ride from the airport into
the city centre costs 600–1000
Kč. There are several buses and
shuttle services to the airport. The
easiest way is probably the airport
bus from Dejvice – Prague 6
[Metro station Dejvická (Line A)].

Railway Stations in Prague

Central Station (cf. p. 160)
[Hlavní nádraží]
Wilsonova • 120 00 Praha 2
Ⓜ C Hlavní nádraží
*Through station. The main domestic and
international services leave from the Central
Station. Alongside the ticket counters in the
main hall are accommodation bureaus, ex-
change offices, travel agents, newsstands and
restaurants.*

Masaryk Station
[Masarykovo nádraží]
Hybernská • 110 00 Praha 1
Ⓜ B Náměstí Republiky
*Terminus. All domestic trains heading north
or east leave from here.*

Holešovice Station
[Nádraží Holešovice]
Partyzánská • 170 00 Praha 7
Ⓜ C Nádraží Holešovice
*Through station. Trains to Vienna, Dresden,
Berlin and Hamburg leave from here. As
well as ticket offices, there are accommoda-
tion bureaus, exchange offices and shops sell-
ing travel accessories in the main hall.*

Smíchov Station [Smíchovské nádraží]
Nádražní • 150 00 Praha 5
Ⓜ B Smíchovské nádraží
Through station. Some domestic and international trains stop here before going on to the Central Station. Trains to Castle Karlštejn also leave from here.

Coach Terminals

ČSAD
Křižíkova 4 • 180 00 Praha 8
Phone: 900 144 444 • www.florenc.info
Ⓜ B, C Florenc

ČSAD
autobusové stanoviště Holešovice
170 00 Praha 7 • www.uan.cz
Ⓜ C Nádraží Holešovice

Getting Around by Car

Drivers need to carry a green international insurance card in addition to their national licence as well as a set of spare bulbs. Vehicles whose number plates do not include a European Union country code must have a separate country code sticker.

Seatbelts are absolutely obligatory and there is a zero tolerance policy towards driving while intoxicated; helmets are compulsory for motorcyclists. Headlights must always be switched on.

The speed limit is 50 kph within city limits, 90 kph on open roads and 130 kph on motorways.

Trams always have right of way while turning off!

Most of the motorways and expressways are subject to fees. The road tax stickers (vignettes) are available at the border crossings, at post offices and at petrol stations. Vignettes can be bought for a week, a month or a year.

If caught speeding or breaking any other rules, it is advisable not to argue with the officer – it could easily become even more expensive!

Parking

When parking, always ensure that the road remains unobstructed for a width of at least 3 metres. Waiting or parking is forbidden on bridges as well as 15 m before and after train crossings, tunnels and subways. A yellow line on the road means no parking.

In the centre of Prague, most parking lots are for residents only (marked with a "P" and a blue line); offenders may expect steep fines. Prague police officers are true virtuosos in fitting wheel clamps [botičky] with incredible speed, so it is better to refrain from unauthorized parking. If you still decide to take a chance and get caught out, call the number on the note left on your windscreen and wait (quite frequently more than an hour) for the police patrol to come back and, after due payment, remove the clamp. Here too, arguing is generally counterproductive. Besides, it could have

Prague police at work.

been worse: The City Police tows away illegally parked cars within minutes with a crane truck. To find out where to pick up the car, enquire by phone or at the nearest police station. Naturally, information is only available after the payment of a considerable fine.

To avoid all of this, you would do better to head for one of the secured parking lots (such as the one right next to the Central Station) or one of the slightly more expensive parking levels (at the Kotva department store on náměstí Republiky or the underground carpark at the Rudolfinum for example).

Car Hire

A valid passport and driver's license must be produced on renting a car.

AVIS Rent A Car
Praha City Centre
Klimentská 46 • 110 02 Praha 1
Phone: 221 851 225-6 • www.avis.cz
Ⓣ 3, 26 TĚŠNOV

A Rent Car
Millenium Plaza
V Celnici 10 • 110 00 Praha 1
Phone: 224 211 587 • www.arentcar.cz
Ⓜ B NÁMĚSTÍ REPUBLIKY

Hertz – Airport Ruzyně
Aviatická • Parking C • 160 00 Praha 6
Phone: 225 345 021 • www.hertz.cz
Ⓜ A DEJVICKÁ, then change to Ⓑ "Airport bus"

Phone calls in the Czech Republic

Most of the telephone boxes in the centre are operated with phone cards [*telefonní karty*] that can be bought at post offices, newsstands and tobacconists [*trafika*]. International calls from a land line are cheaper if you dial 970 before the country code.

Important Numbers

Ambulance	155
Police (emergency)	158
City Police	156
Fire Brigade	150
Doctors (on call)	183
Pharmacies (24-hour)	184
Domestic Directory Assistance	1180
International Directory Assistance	1181
24-hour Breakdown Service	1230

Country Codes

Austria	0043
Czech Republic	00420
France	0033
Germany	0049
Great Britain	0044
Italy	0039
Japan	0081
Poland	0048
Russia	007
Spain	0034
Switzerland	0041
USA	001

Train Information
840 112 113 www.cd.cz

Flight Connections
239 007 007 www.csa.cz

Bus, Train and Flight Connections
www.jizdnirady.cz idos3@chaps.cz

Travelling with Children

Baby care facilities or services are fairly uncommon in hotels and restaurants. Some hotels offer a babysitter service. Children are often welcome in restaurants. Children's dishes are sometimes offered on the menu, smaller helpings can usually be made to order.

Is there anything for kids around here?

Things Children Love:

Divadlo minor
Vodičkova 6 • 110 00 Praha 1
Phone: 222 231 702 • www.minor.cz
Ⓣ 3, 9, 14, 24 VODIČKOVA
Puppet theatre, often with live music.

Divadlo Spejbla a Hurvínka
Dejvická 38 • 160 00 Praha 6
Phone: 224 316 784
www.spejbl-hurvinek.cz
Ⓜ A DEJVICKÁ
World-famous puppet theatre, telling stories about father Spejbl and his son Hurvínek.

Horse-drawn Carriages
A relatively inexpensive treat for young and old alike. Ride through Prague city centre in a horse-drawn carriage, driven by a true Prague coachman. Departures are from the Old Town Square.

Boat Cruises, Rowing Boats or Pedal Boats on the Vltava
Boat hire:
Slovanský ostrov • 110 00 Praha 1
Ⓣ 6, 9, 17, 18, 21, 22 NÁRODNÍ DIVADLO

Mirror Maze on Petřín Hill (cf. p. 100)
Petřínské sady • 118 00 Praha 1
Phone: 257 315 212
Ⓣ 6, 9, 12, 20, 22 ÚJEZD, then change to the funicular [Lanovka]

Toy Museum (see under "museums")

A Tram Ride on Nostalgic Line 91
You can get on at the following stops: Výstaviště, Veletržní, Strossmayerovo náměstí, Nábřeží kapitána Jaroše, Čechův most, Malostranská, Malostranské náměstí, Hellichova, Újezd, Národní divadlo, Národní třída, Lazarská, Vodičkova, Václavské náměstí, Jindřišská, Masarykovo nádraží, Náměstí Republiky, Dlouhá třída.

Tramway Museum (see under "museums")

Sparky's Dům hraček
Havířská 2 • 110 00 Praha 1
Phone: 224 239 309 • www.sparkys.cz
Ⓜ A, B MŮSTEK
Prague's biggest toy shop.

Prague Zoo
U Trojského zámku 3 • 171 00 Praha 7
Phone: 296 112 111 • www.zoopraha.cz
Ⓜ C NÁDRAŽÍ HOLEŠOVICE, then change to
Ⓑ 112 ZOOLOGICKÁ ZAHRADA
Established in 1931, the zoo spreads out over extensive rocky grounds. It is famous for the rare Przewalski's horses, with a small funicular leading up to their enclosure.

Speibl and Hurvínek.

Prague Zoo.

Playgrounds

There is a large playground on Children's Island [Dětský ostrov, Ⓣ 6, 9, 12, 20 ARBESOVO NÁMĚSTÍ] as well as on Letná, close to the metronome (Ⓣ 18, 20 CHOTKOVY SADY). The surrounding park also offers a lot of opportunities for play and sporting activites like jogging, roller skating and skateboarding.

Lost Property Office

Ztráty a nálezy • Karoliny Světlé 5
110 00 Praha 1 • Phone: 224 235 085
Ⓣ 6, 9, 17, 18, 21, 22 NÁRODNÍ DIVADLO

Customs Offices in Prague

There are very few export restrictions on goods for personal use, however, some antiques or objets d'art may require an export licence.

Customs office at the central station
(see under railway stations)

Customs office at Ruzyně Airport
Aviatická 12 • 160 08 Praha 6
Phone: 220 113 100 • www.cs.mfcr.cz
Ⓜ A DEJVICKÁ, then change to Ⓑ "Airport bus"

Main Customs Office Prague
Plzeňská 139 • 150 00 Praha 5
Phone: 257 019 111 • www.cs.mfcr.cz
Ⓣ 4, 7, 9, 10 KLAMOVKA

Fact Sheet

Total Area	497 km² (191.51 sq mi)
Population	1.2 million
Elevation	177–397 m (581–1,309 ft) above sea level
Administration	22 boroughs, 57 districts
Economy	The most important seat of industry in the

Czech Republic. Tourism is one of Prague's main economic assets alongside engineering and vehicle manufacturing, oil refinery and electrical, textile, printing and chemical industries.

Sports

There are always between two and four Prague football clubs in the Czech first division (1. Liga); this means that there is a home game almost every weekend. The best known clubs outside the Czech Republic are Sparta and Slavia, however, Viktoria Žižkov is also very popular in Prague.

Ultimately though, the Czech national sport is ice hockey. The entire nation follows every twist and turn of the various championships, rooting for their "hockeyists" on TV or in sports bars.

An informative website for English-speaking expats in Prague is www.expats.cz, which also serves as a forum for all aspects of life in the city. The site gives up-to-date information on sports facilities, fitness centres etc. Anyone looking for a suitable sports partner, be it a tennis coach, a volleyball team or a trekking companion, would do well to start here.

Cycling

Avid cyclists will take to the pedals anywhere, even in Prague. But with few cycle lanes, insane traffic, bumpy cobblestones and a rather hilly terrain, the city on the Vltava isn't exactly a cyclist's paradise. In fact, a bicycle is probably not a very practical mode of transport in the city. Moreover, cyclists tend to be regarded as rather eccentric in this city of car lovers. No politician here would ever think of showing the common touch by cycling to work. Where Jaguar and Mercedes are status symbols, you won't score many points with a boneshaker.

Swimming

Swim Stadium Podolí
Podolská 74 • 140 00 Praha 4
Phone: 241 433 952
Ⓣ 3, 16, 17, 21 Kublov

All about Money

1 Czech Crown = 100 Hellers
Coins: 1, 2, 5, 10, 20
             and 50 Crowns.
Banknotes: 50, 100, 200, 500, 1000,
             2000 and 5000 Crowns.

Banks will usually offer better exchange rates than bureaux de change. You can also simply withdraw money from an ATM, however some banks will charge a service fee. Travellers' cheques in Euros or US Dollars are accepted by banks, bureaux de change, large shops and hotels. Euros and US Dollars are rarely accepted in shops. Most shops, restaurants, hotels and car hire firms will, however, accept credit cards. Changing money with hawkers is always inadvisable.

Shopping

Wenceslas Square is a good starting point for a shopping trip. "In the Moat" [Na Příkopě] and Paris Street [Pařížská] are probably the best known shopping streets in Prague, dominated by established (and pricy) brand names: Louis Vuitton, Dior and Burberry, Hugo Boss, Cartier and Swarovski. The pedestrian precincts at Karlová, Celetná and Mostecká can feel like the world capital of tourist trash:

Bohemian Garnets.

ham and powidl (plum jam) – the latter is mainly found in supermarkets. The latest ranges of Moravian shoe company Baťa are available in the Baťa department store on Wenceslas Square; the textile producer Hedva, also based in Moravia, sells its wares on Na Příkopě.

Shopaholics will find numerous shopping arcades and centres tucked away down little alleys and behind old façades, the "Myslbek" centre and the "Shopping Center Černá Růže" on Na Příkopě or the "Lucerna Arcade" on Vodičkova Street for example. Anyone looking for Czech fashion should head to the long-established "OP Prostějov Profashion".

closely packed rows of shops that all look exactly the same, all selling kitschy glass figurines, trinkets and embarrassing T-shirts ("Czech it out", "Prague Drinking Team"). Amongst all this, there seems to have been a population explosion of Russian Matryoshka stacking dolls (counted as "Slavic art").

Bohemian glass is a popular souvenir of the Czech Republic, as are jewellery, children's toys, antiques, Carlsbad spa wafers, Becherovka (a green bitters), Prague

There are all kinds of curiosities waiting for a buyer in Prague's many antique shops. Be careful though: much is overpriced, some items may be fakes or damaged.

Hot dog stand on Wenceslas Square.

Czech-made toys.

There is no law governing the hours of trading in the Czech Republic, so many shops are open at the weekend, while some do business 24/7. If all that shopping gives you an appetite, there are plenty of hotdog stands, especially on Wenceslas Square; a fat juicy "Klobasa", for example, might hit the spot. Maybe that smart suit or that elegant dress should have been a size larger after all …

Czech Folk Art
Mostecka 13 • 110 00 Praha 1
Ⓣ 12, 20, 22 Malostranské náměstí
One of the innumerable souvenir shops selling wooden toys, clothes, pottery, wrought-iron work and painted Easter eggs – in stock the whole year round.

Dům obuvi Baťa [House of Shoes]
Václavské náměstí 6 • 110 00 Praha 1
Ⓜ A, B Můstek
Fashionable shoes for ladies, gentlemen and children; sport and leisure shoes, accessories,
various leather goods. The kids' corner on the second floor is always popular!

Hedva
Na Příkopě 16 • 110 00 Praha 1
Ⓜ A, B Můstek
This shop sells Czech-made handkerchiefs and ties, made from natural silk or polyester, in classic or modern designs.

Neoluxor Palace of Books
Václavské náměstí 41 • 110 00 Praha 1
Phone: 221 111 370 • www.neoluxor.cz
Ⓜ A, B Můstek
Books galore right on Wenceslas Square. Internet access is available downstairs.

Obchod pod Lampou
U Lužického semináře 5/78
110 00 Praha 1
Ⓣ 12, 20, 22 Malostranské náměstí
In the shadow of Charles Bridge, the shop "Beneath the Lamp" sells hand-carved puppets with costumes sewn on the premises.

OP Prostějov Profashion
Vodičkova 33 • 110 00 Praha 1
Ⓜ A, B Můstek
Czech-made suits, dresses, fashion jeans and evening wear (also sold under the label "Bernhardt").

mostly taken up with the larger chains, cafés and restaurants; underground car park.

Paneria bakeries
Dlouha 50 • 110 00 Praha 1
Ⓣ 5, 8, 14 Dlouhá
As in many other branches of the large chain of bakeries, (Národní, Vítězná, Kaprova ...) a wide range of refreshments such as sandwiches, cakes, muffins and coffee is offered. Everything is also available to take away.

Markets

Old Town Square
Staroměstské náměstí • 110 00 Praha 1
Ⓜ A Staroměstská
Twice a year, the Old Town Square becomes a marketplace: Handicrafts, some endearing and others useless, are offered for sale before Easter and Christmas. Fried sausage, beer and mulled wine are readily available.

Havelský trh
Havelská • 110 00 Praha 1
Ⓜ A, B Můstek
One of the oldest weekly markets in the city with fruit and vegetables at good prices, as well as wooden toys, handicrafts and jewellery (occasionally somewhat overpriced).

Vitalis Bookstore
U Lužického semináře 19 • 118 00 Praha 1
www.vitalis-verlag.com
Ⓜ A Malostranská
Small bookstore offering a wide selection of foreign language books and special rates for titles published in-house by Vitalis. Settle down on a nostalgic sofa and bury yourself in a book!

Palladium shopping centre
náměstí Republiky 1 • 110 00 Praha 1
Phone: 225 770 250
www.palladiumpraha.cz
Ⓜ B Náměstí Republiky
Opened in 2007 and currently the largest shopping centre in Prague. Five floors are

The Palladium shopping mall.

Fresh vegetables on Prague's markets.

The Motol University Hospital.

Holešovická tržnice
Bubenské nábřeží • 170 00 Praha 7
Ⓜ C Vltavská
This former slaughterhouse is now home to a market selling all kinds of industrial products, assorted jumble and many snack stalls.

There are several other markets in big parking lots on the outskirts, where traders, often Vietnamese, have stalls of consumer goods including fake designer clothes, cheap liquor, garden gnomes, various electronic items and so on.

Medical Care for Foreigners

There are some international hospitals and doctor's surgeries in Prague where treatment is available in the more common foreign languages. In general, medical standards in the capital are on an international level.

University Hospital
[Všeobecná fakultní nemocnice v Praze]
U Nemocnice 2/Ecke Karlovo náměstí
128 08 Praha 2 • Phone: 224 961 111
www.vfn.cz
Ⓜ B Karlovo náměstí
Large hospital complex belonging to the medical faculty, with public clinics, research institutes, laboratories and walk-in clinics.

Motol University Hospital
[Fakultní nemocnice v Motole]
V úvalu 84 • 150 06 Praha 5
Phone: 224 431 111 • www.fnmotol.cz
Ⓑ 167, 174, 179, 180, 184 Nemocnice Motol
Large, modern hospital with a department for foreigners, where English, German, French, Russian and Spanish is spoken.

Motol University Hospital
[Nemocnice Na Homolce]
Roentgenova 2 • 150 30 Praha 5
Phone: 257 271 111 • www.homolka.cz
Ⓑ 167 Nemocnice Na Homolce
Hospital with a good reputation and a department with English-speaking doctors. In close proximity to Motol University Hospital.

24-Hour Pharmacies

Lékárna Nemocnice Na Františku
Palackého 5 • 110 00 Praha 1
Phone: 224 946 982
Ⓣ 3, 9, 14, 24 Vodičkova

Lékárna U Anděla
Štefánikova 250/6 • 150 00 Praha 5
Phone: 257 320 194
Ⓜ B Anděl

Post Offices and Postal Charges

Post boxes are painted orange in Prague and always indicate when they will be next emptied. A letter within the EU is generally delivered within two to four days;

it takes 5 to 10 days to the rest of the world. As you may not be able to buy stamps along with your postcards, you should expect to make a trip to the nearest post office.

24-Hour Post Office
Jindřišská 14 • 110 00 Praha 1
Phone: 221 131 111 • www.cpost.cz
Information Centre: 800 104 410
Ⓜ A, B MŮSTEK

Postal Charges

Domestic up to 50g (Postcards and letters)	10 Kč
EU up to 20g (Postcards and letters)	17 Kč
EU up to 50g	21 Kč
Overseas up to 20g (Postcards and letters)	18 Kč
Overseas up to 50g	24 Kč

Guided Tours and Daytrips

There are various guided tours of the city which can be useful either to get an initial overview or to learn more on specific topics (e.g. Franz Kafka and Prague, music in Prague, mystical Prague). Groups meet several times a day at the Astronomical Clock in the Old Town Square and may be joined for a fee.

For more information (in English, German and Spanish), refer to www.walks.cz.

Church Services in Foreign Languages

There are church services for visitors held in most common foreign languages. Catholic masses are most common but there are also Protestant, Orthodox, Baptist and Anglican services. Jewish services are mostly read in Hebrew, but there are also Czech and English services in the Spanish Synagogue. There are Rabbis from conservative, orthodox and reformed congregations.

English Services:

International Church of Prague (Evangelical)
Peroutkova 57 • 150 00 Praha 5
Sundays 10.30 a.m.
Phone: 296 392 338
www.internationalchurchofprague.cz
Ⓜ B ANDĚL, then change to Ⓑ 137, 501 UR-BANOVA

St Thomas' Church (Roman Catholic)
Josefská 8 • 118 00 Praha 1
Saturdays 6 p.m., Sundays 11 a.m.
Ⓣ 12, 20, 22 MALOSTRANSKÉ NÁMĚSTÍ

St Clement's Church (Anglican)
Klimentská 5 • 1100 00 Praha 1
Sundays 11 a.m.
Ⓣ 5, 8, 14, 51, 54 DLOUHÁ TŘÍDA

Jewish Services
www.kehilaprag.cz

Old-New Synagogue (cf. p. 149)
Červená 2 • 110 00 Praha 1
Weekdays 8 a.m., Sundays 9 a.m.
Fridays and Saturdays after sunset (service is in Hebrew)
Ⓜ A STAROMĚSTSKÁ

Spanish Synagogue (cf. p. 152)
Dušní • 110 00 Praha 1
Saturdays 10 a.m., Fridays and Saturdays after sunset (Friday services are also in English and Czech)
Ⓜ A STAROMĚSTSKÁ

Index